CHRISTIAN EDUCATION AS EVANGELISM

CHRISTIAN EDUCATION AS EVANGELISM

Edited by Norma Cook Everist

FORTRESS PRESS

MINNEAPOLIS

CHRISTIAN EDUCATION AS EVANGELISM

Contributors to this volume are professors of Christian Education at the seminaries of the Evangelical Lutheran Church in America and the Evangelical Lutheran Church in Canada. Edited by Norma Cook Everist.

Large-quantity purchases or custom editions of this book are available at a discount from the publisher. For more information, contact the sales department at Augsburg Fortress, Publishers, 1-800-328-4648, or write to: Sales Director, Augsburg Fortress, Publishers, Box 1209, Minneapolis, MN 55440-1209.

Cover design by Dave Meyer
Main cover photo © Denis Felix/Taxi/Getty Images. Used by permission.
Small cover photo © Don Farrall/Photodisc Green/Getty Images.
Book design by Michelle L. N. Cook

Library of Congress Cataloging-in-Publication Data

Libray of Congress Cataloging-in-Publication data available.

ISBN 978-0-8006-6213-4

The paper used in this publication meets the minimum requirements of American National Standard for Information Sciences—Permanence of Paper for Printed Library Materials, ANSI Z329.48-1984.

Manufactured in the U.S.A.

11   10   09   08   07   1   2   3   4   5   6   7   8   9   10

TABLE OF CONTENTS

117860

Part Three: Claiming the Challenge

CONTRIBUTORS

Chapter 1

Diane J. Hymans is Professor of Christian Education and Associate Academic Dean at Trinity Lutheran Seminary in Columbus, Ohio, where she teaches courses in educational ministry, children and the church, youth ministry, and media and education in the congregation. In addition, she serves as codirector of the Center for Educational Ministry in the Parish. One of her favorite jobs is serving as teacher of the fourth- and fifth-grade Sunday school class in her local Presbyterian congregation.

Chapter 2

Margaret A. Krych is Associate Dean of Graduate Education and Charles F. Norton Professor of Christian Education and Theology at the Lutheran Theological Seminary at Philadelphia. An ordained ELCA pastor, she directs the seminary's advanced level degree programs and has taught Christian education for more than thirty years. Among her publications is the book *Teaching the Gospel Today*. She belongs to a congregation known for outreach and mission along with a vibrant Christian education program for people of all ages.

Chapter 3

Carol R. Jacobson is Assistant Professor of Practical Theology: Youth and Family Ministries at Pacific Lutheran Theological Seminary in Berkeley, California. She teaches courses in systematic theology, Christian education, and youth ministry. She also directs the Life Together program, which offers theological education for high school youth on the seminary campus. She is a member of Resurrection Lutheran Church in Oakland, California.

Chapter 4

Donald R. Just is Coordinator for Ministry Education in Region Four of the Evangelical Lutheran Church in America. It is a deployed staff position in the ELCA's Vocation and Education Unit. He is an ordained pastor in the ELCA. He has served as a parish pastor, military chaplain, campus pastor and, until 2006, as Adjunct Professor of Educational Ministry and Liturgy at the Lutheran Seminary Program in the Southwest in Austin, Texas.

Chapter 5

Mary E. Hughes is Professor of Christian Education at Trinity Lutheran Seminary in Columbus, Ohio. She is Director of the Master of Arts in Lay Ministry and Master of Theological Studies degree programs and codirector of the Center for Educational Ministry in the Parish. A Lutheran lay person specializing in adult education, she is committed to equipping those in the church's non-ordained ministries.

Chapter 6

Eddie K. Kwok is Assistant Professor of Christian Education and Mission at the Lutheran Theological Seminary in Saskatoon, Saskatchawan. An ordained pastor of the Evangelical Lutheran Church in Canada, he has served on the Missions Committee of the British Columbia Synod and the Canadian Missions Working Group. Along with his teaching responsibilities, he also liaises between the church and the Chinese community. His passions include intercultural studies and globalization.

Chapter 7

Nelson T. Strobert is Professor of Christian Education and Director of Multicultural Programs at the Lutheran Theological Seminary at Gettysburg in Pennsylvania. He is a pastor of the ELCA and has served congregations in Saint Croix, U.S. Virgin Islands and in Cleveland, Ohio. He is a member of Curriculum Conversations Relating Theory and Practice of the National Council of Churches of Christ and the Conference of International Black Lutherans (CIBL). His research interests include curriculum history, Lutheran parochial education, multicultural education, and educational biography.

Chapter 8

Phyllis N. Kersten is Associate Pastor at Grace Lutheran Church in River Forest, Illinois. A former teacher, she became an ELCA pastor in 1996 and has served at Grace—a congregation with a multifaceted educational ministry—ever since. She has served as adjunct faculty at the Lutheran School of Theology at Chicago, teaching Educational Ministry in the Parish. She is coauthor of several women's Bible studies, including the 1990 Women of the ELCA study, and of R Is for Religion, a children's curriculum.

Chapter 9

Mary E. Hess is Associate Professor of Educational Leadership at Luther Seminary in Saint Paul, Minnesota. A Roman Catholic layperson, her interests focus around questions of congregational mission and religious education within digital cultural contexts. She is a member of the International Study Commission on Media, Religion and Culture, and her most recent book is entitled *Engaging Technology in Theological Education: All that We Can't Leave Behind.*

Chapter 10

Kristine A. Lund is Assistant Professor of Contextual Ministry and Pastoral Counseling at Waterloo Lutheran Seminary, Waterloo, Ontario. An ordained pastor in the Evangelical Lutheran Church in Canada and a Specialist and Teaching Supervisor in Pastoral Counseling, she is interested in the experience of teaching and learning in both the therapeutic and pastoral relationship.

Chapter 11

Norma Cook Everist is Professor of Educational Ministry and Church Administration at Wartburg Theological Seminary, Dubuque, Iowa. A Lutheran deaconess and an ELCA pastor, she served parish communities in Saint Louis, Missouri; Detroit, Michigan; and New Haven, Connecticut, before teaching at Yale Divinity School and, for the past twenty-eight years, at Wartburg. Her most recent books are *Transforming Leadership* (with Craig Nessan), and *Open the Doors and See All the People: Stories of Congregation Identity and Vocation.*

Chapter 12

Susan Wilds McArver is Associate Professor of Educational Ministry and Church History at Lutheran Theological Southern Seminary, Columbia, South Carolina, where she also serves as Director of the Center on Religion in the South. Her research interests include the intersections of religious history and faith formation. Her most recent publication is *A Goodly Heritage: The Story of Lutheran Theological Southern Seminary 1830–2005,* coauthored with Scott Hendrix. She is an active lay member of Incarnation Lutheran Church, Columbia.

CHRISTIAN EDUCATION AND EVANGELISM: TWO SIDES OF THE SAME COIN

Thomas H. Groome

I am honored to write the foreword for this fine set of essays. That I, a Catholic, would be so invited by a group of scholars teaching at Lutheran Seminaries in the United States and Canada signals progress by the Christian Church toward the unity among disciples for which Jesus prayed earnestly (John 17:21).

Unity through uniformity, however, would not be an achievement; in fact, it would diminish the richness of the Body of Christ. Instead, as Christian persons and communities, we are called to "unity with diversity," to a deep bond in faith while being enriched by an array of different charisms and particular traditions.

This collection is a fine instance of wisdom that arises from a specific Christian community—Lutherans—that will be a gift to the whole Church. Unlike modernity that so favored meta-narratives, thus fostering sectarianism, postmodern consciousness seems more likely to encourage such distinctive expressions from people's "own stories" of faith. For sure, all of our traditions will contribute most fruitfully to the universal Church from our own particularity. Case in point, this collection by professors at Lutheran Seminaries will surely find relevance and resonance among "neighbors" in the Body of Christ as well.

Of late, my Catholic community has officially embraced the position that evangelization is the key to catechesis (the Catholic preferred terms), that all efforts to educate in faith must promote Christian discipleship—apprenticeship to Jesus. For example, the *General Directory for Catechesis* (1997) proposes that the primary catechetical purpose is "to put people . . . in communion and intimacy with Jesus Christ" (#80), to promote "full and sincere adherence to his person and the decision to walk in his footsteps" (#53). After many centuries (since the Reformation) of emphasizing doctrinal accuracy, this prioritizing of discipleship, making evangelization the key to catechesis, comes as welcome to Catholic Christians.

Regarding the interface of Christian education and evangelism (the Protestant preferred terms), this collection, however, makes exactly the reverse proposal—that the key to evangelism is Christian education. I'm totally convinced that the Church needs both equations, because Christian education and evangelism are two sides of the same coin. Indeed, all Christian education should evangelize, but conversely, evangelism can bear lasting fruit only when sustained by good Christian education.

I'm taking evangelism to mean the proclamation of Jesus Christ as Lord and Savior, calling people to discipleship, and their initial encounter with and embrace of Christian faith. But such conversion typically takes place through Christian nurture and requires that the person become informed, formed, and constantly transformed toward the holiness of life demanded of disciples. In other words, to be realized—incarnated—in people's lives, evangelism to Christian faith demands good education.

Even if conversion is achieved through some life changing occurrence, the person so blessed will still need Christian education to mature in faith and grow in holiness. Paul's becoming a Christian was catalyzed by his Damascus road experience. But then he needed a community in Damascus of "men and women who belonged to the Way" (Acts 9: 2) to begin his formation in Christian identity; thereafter, he still had his "race to run" (2 Tim. 4:7). Evangelism always needs lifelong Christian education.

Of course, we must move away from the stereotypes that evangelism is the exciting and jazzy enterprise whereas Christian education is humdrum and boring. This arises, in part, from making Christian education synonymous with schooling—of some kind. In fact, effective Christian education requires the socializing power of every aspect of family and congregational life, as well as formal programs of instruction. And the latter should be crafted around participative and conversational pedagogies that enable people, cradle to grave, to bring their lives to Christian faith and Christian faith to their daily lives. Nothing could be more exciting!

This collection will help to promote such holistic Christian education. Insofar as people embrace and implement its proposals, they will have the key to evangelism.

Thomas H. Groome is Professor of Theology and Religious Education at Boston College and Director of BC's Institute of Religious Education and Pastoral Ministry.

INTRODUCTION

Education leads to evangelism and evangelism leads to education. It must be so! It is so! Theologian and educator Letty Russell wrote in one of her earliest books, *Christian Education in Mission,* that the Christian community is a witnessing community, gathered together by the love of Christ, which is too wonderful not to be shared in words, actions and service. Christian community is the context for Christian education. When invitation to join in God's mission is not lived out "and the community is not a *witnessing* community, those who are being nurtured in the community receive 'miseducation' or a gift of education that has already been turned into a stone."[1]

The mission statement at Wartburg Theological Seminary invites people to: "A place where learning leads to mission and mission informs learning."[2] Or, to put it another way, "learning leads to mission leads to mission leads to learning. . . ."[3] While each of the terms "evangelism," "mission," and "outreach" has unique connotations, and the ministry of "education" goes by many names, the calling, the connection, and the commitment are the same: education leads to evangelism, which leads to education, which leads to evangelism. . . . It must be so! It is so!

Why, then, have evangelism and education so often been pitted against one another in budgets, time, and energy? Sometimes an emphasis on Christian education is interpreted as "living in the past" while evangelism is promised to be the "way of the future." Sometimes one hears it is said that education is "soft" or "boring," that which happens in the church basement to people already inside the church, whereas evangelism is "new, strong, and exciting," that which reaches outside. On the other side of the divide, some people faithfully cling to education in the church but fear evangelism, even flee the calling, thereby also setting evangelism and education against each other. These false dichotomies, these erroneous images, do justice to neither education nor evangelism.

If the Evangelical Lutheran Church in America (ELCA) and the Evangelical Lutheran Church in Canada (ELCIC) and many other church bodies are to carry out their goals of evangelical outreach, solid teaching is necessary. If church bodies are to faithfully educate, they must provide teaching and learning ministries that are alive and that spring forth into a vital sharing of the good news of Jesus Christ. This book shows how we can build on our Reformation foundations to reach out to all kinds of people with the gospel in a pluralistic world. The education and evangelism connection leads to vocation: a calling of all the baptized.

The Book and Its Authors

This book was born through an exciting conversation in the fall of 2005 in Toronto, Ontario. Professors of Christian education at seminaries of the ELCA and the ELCIC met for two days preceding the annual meeting of the Religious Education Association.

The professors were discussing, *Our Calling in Education: A Lutheran Study,*[4] the first publication of the ELCA Task Force on Education. That study and the subsequent first draft of a social statement[5] were disseminated across the church body in preparation for the ELCA Churchwide Assembly in Chicago in 2007. The ELCA in assembly in 2003 adopted "A Vision for Evangelism in the Evangelical Lutheran Church in America."[6] Two of the objectives of the ELCA Evangelism Strategy are "to prepare and renew evangelical leaders" and to "teach discipleship."

The Evangelical Lutheran Church in Canada approved "The Evangelical Declaration" at its National Convention in 1997. It includes this statement: "We commit ourselves as church to equip all of us to be people in mission and life as faithful disciples. We will emphasize ongoing learning for both laity and clergy. We will make full use of the resources of the people in our congregations, schools, seminaries and leadership positions in the church."[7] The Rev. Paul N. Johnson, ELCIC Assistant to the Bishop for Ecumenical Relations, Lutheran Communion, Mission in the World and Worship, said, "The link is clear, sharing the good news of Jesus Christ—evangelism—belongs with Christian education as word and melody join to form hymns of thankful praise."[8]

That vibrant conversation among professors of Christian education in Toronto by the end of the first evening had turned into a commitment to write a book connecting education and evangelism. Bill Huff, who was present at the meeting representing Augsburg Fortress, fully endorsed the idea and encouraged publication to coincide with the ELCA Churchwide Assembly in 2007. The final chapter of this book, *Christian Education as Evangelism,* is written by Professor Susan Wilds McArver, of Lutheran Theological Southern Seminary, who also is a member of the Task Force on Education. She was able to include the final work by the Task Force as they sent their report to the ELCA Church Council in the spring of 2007.

This is the fifth book—all published by Augsburg Fortress —written by Christian Education Professors in Lutheran seminaries. The first book, *Education for Christian Living* (1987), emphasized the comprehensive calling of Christian Education in the parish. The second, *Lifelong Learning* (1997), focused on the exciting, challenging calling of adult education. The third, *Confirmation: Engaging Lutheran Foundations and Practices* (1999), laid theological and educational grounding for the church's confirmation ministry. The fourth, *The Ministry of Children's Education* (2004), once again focused on a specific age group, looking at the child developmentally and theologically, and providing a wealth of ideas for educational ministry among children.

In each of these collaborative endeavors the professors functioned as a team. The authors are delighted that once again—as in the first book—authorship includes professors of the

Canadian seminaries, embodying the close connection between the ELCIC and the ELCA. Over this twenty year span, as one would expect, some professors retired and others took their places. But the collaborative spirit continues, not unlike the church itself, working together educationally through the years. In this book, each of the twelve professors wrote one chapter on a topic directly related to the subject of connecting evangelism and education for the lively mission of the churches.

What Is the Connection?

There are many dynamics to these terms "education" and "evangelism." Certainly education leads to evangelism and evangelism leads to education in many ways.

What is evangelism? What is education? What is the connection? There are multi-faceted answers. The authors have diverse ideas. Likewise readers also will have differing responses to those questions. Diverse views are welcome!

Evangelism, in a broad and deep sense, means reaching out to everyone with good news. This means being an evangelizing community through the means of grace, knowing the pain of the cross and the power of the resurrection, and fully utilizing the ministry of all the baptized.[9] People need Christian education that provides a real encounter with the Word of God and with one another. As God's people engage the scriptures, the scriptures engage them, entering their whole lives. Nothing is left outside. We come together around the Word as we are, living in the midst of the human predicament that is in need of God's unconditional love in Jesus Christ. By the power of the Spirit we are transformed and sent forth, equipped for service and to become courageous workers for justice and healers of humanity in a global community. Christian education itself becomes gospel good news when done well.

Christian education as evangelism reaches children, youth, and adults of every age. How can the entire congregation become transformed to think of itself as an educating and evangelizing parish? How does education build disciples who are able to connect faith with their ministries in daily life? Education is key to helping people re-enter the Church after having been away for many years.

Christian Education is itself "good news" to faith communities where biblical literacy and faith knowledge is low. In order to reach people who have never known the love of Jesus Christ, and to reach people at various stages of faith development, we must listen well in order to know where they are in their perspectives on life and concepts of God. What educational opportunities can the church offer in the community, from early childhood centers to lay schools of theology? The evangelical challenge of education is to reach new people and also to re-evangelize by helping people remember, reclaim, and renew their faith. In today's society, Christian people may know what they are against but not what they are for. Congregation members (not just confirmands) should be able to articulate their own statement of faith in order to share their faith with others. Life-long learning is an ongoing evangelical vocation.

Education and evangelism are closely and vitally linked. All Christian education must be parish neighborhood education. Education is measured in evangelical mission.

The Chapters: Questions, Possibilities and Challenges

Each author has a distinct voice, distinct views, including about the nature of education and evangelism, but their purposes are the same. Each author has a different style of writing, different background, life experience, and geographical location, but their commitments are united.

Part One: Embracing the Questions

In chapter 1 Diane J. Hymans explores the question of the essential education evangelism connection. She carefully examines the various meanings of "education" as "teaching and learning," "faith formation," "nurture," "discipleship," "life experience," and "schooling." To engage in education is to be in intentional conversation in relationship with other teachers and learners about experience as the people of God in light of the church's tradition.

In chapter 2 Margaret A. Krych writes that one is hard pressed to know whether the Reformation was an effort in re-evangelization or education. She grounds the connection theologically. Using the work of Paul Tillich, she shows the gospel message has two sides, one of human need that reveals people's pretenses before God, and the other the incredibly good news of God's love and merciful forgiveness. This needs to be taught to those who have never heard it and to those who vaguely know it and need to hear it again and to understand it.

In chapter 3 Carol R. Jacobson shows that heart, soul, mind, and strength are all involved in knowing the power and the promise of the gospel. Christian education recognizes and celebrates the involvement of the entire self in the practices of learning to know the gospel. Christian educational practices are always operating on cognitive, affective, and active levels. In this way the gospel is made alive in individuals and in the hearts and minds of the community.

In chapter 4 Donald R. Just, reminiscing from his long experience in ministry, concludes that while most Christians assume that sharing and proclaiming the faith is an essential part of being a disciple, not many would say they have the "gift" for evangelism. He asks not only, "Why is evangelism not happening?" but "Why evangelism?" Just calls for transformative educational experiences so that people cannot help but tell the story of a faithful God's unconditional love in Jesus Christ.

Part Two: Exploring the Possibilities

In chapter 5 Mary E. Hughes explores the many ways that education and evangelism make good partners. Through stories, and interpretation of those stories, she shows congregations, large and small, learning and relearning the basics of the Bible, becoming more skilled in talking about their faith journey at work and at home, more comfortably reaching out to people in their neighborhood, and being genuinely welcoming and hospitable. Outreach and education begin within one's own context.

In chapter 6 Eddie K. Kwok shows educational and evangelizing ministry among Chinese immigrants in western Canada. He points to the importance of people encountering the living Christ as they experience and hear the gospel. The challenge of Christian education in a multicultural context calls for the renewal of the Church to become truly the Church in an increasingly globalized world. Kwok emphasizes the importance of being a hospitable teaching community, one that creates space for others.

In chapter 7 Nelson T. Strobert details how Lutheran early childhood centers, day schools, and high schools are a strong arm of education, often cooperative ventures. School administrators and pastors tell how Lutheran schools can and do reach out beyond the congregation to the community. In addition to general education, they share the gospel of Christ through the formal and implicit curriculum, through worship, and extra-curricular activities, building lasting relationships with students and their families.

In chapter 8 Phyllis N. Kersten encourages congregations to reach out beyond their doors to see the problems and pain, the hungers and longing, and the inequities in the world. Jesus places Christians with one foot in the world and one foot in the Word at the intersection of education and evangelism. The chapter describes bible study specifically tailored to the different learning needs of women and men. Congregations need to listen carefully to the questions about life and the images of the deity that people hold and design learning experiences in response.

Part Three: Claiming the Challenge

In chapter 9 Mary E Hess challenges the church, contending that far too often the impulse to share the good news has been combined with a very narrow definition of teaching and learning. She uses seven languages (Kegan and Lehay) to draw people towards patterns of practice for communities of truth. She asks, "What kind of learning environment creates an active space for listening to God's Word? What kind of teaching designs provide opportunities for such engagement? What kind of learning is transformational? What kind of education is evangelism?"

In chapter 10 Kristine A. Lund challenges churches to effectively minister among young adults, a population with a low formal religious affiliation. Faith for today's young adults is often not faith in a particular religious belief, but rather it is a process of seeking and discovering meaning. "Go and listen" to young adults is the challenge for the church today. They yearn for the divine to be present in their current reality. For many young adults, cyberspace is a place where spirituality and present life meet.

In chapter 11 Norma Cook Everist asks how the church can help people use the "languages" of their daily life, e.g. architecture and agriculture, retail and real estates, to learn and live their faith in their ministries all week. Education and evangelism are translating and transforming experiences. Christian education, if it is to be good news as it relates to people's particular life situation, needs to inquire about the people, their growth in faith, their arenas of daily life, the people to whom *they* speak, and the issues they face in the world.

In chapter 12 Susan Wilds McArver concludes this book by telling the story of the educational process of the ELCA Task Force on Education. Through meetings, hearings, listening posts, forums and individual responses, the task force heard the voices of thousands of people concerned with education in the church. Grounded in Luther's understanding of vocation, our calling is two-fold: "to strive with others to ensure that all have access to a high quality education that develops personal gifts and abilities and serves the common good," and "to educate people in the Christian faith for their vocation" that leads toward discipleship and evangelism.

The book is open-ended in so far as many more topics on Christian education and evangelism could have been included. For instance, particularly in Part Two, "Exploring the Possibilities" chapters could be written about church-affiliated colleges, seminaries, camps and campus ministries, all vital arms of Christian education. The conversation about the connection between education and evangelism continues. Each of the authors developed some facet of that conversation: the questions, the possibilities and the challenges. A theme emerged in many chapters that was unplanned, and yet, in retrospect, not surprising: vocation, the daily life of all the baptized. Christian education must be for all people of all ages; it must be holistic, comprehensive and permeate all of life. Such Christian education equips people to be able to clearly speak their faith in the world in service to the neighbor.

Use of the Book

This book is written for a broad audience. The book is deeply theological and educational, and written in every day language for all to use: directors of Christian education, pastors, diaconal ministers, associates in ministry, church councils, boards and task forces. A Christian Education Committee and an Evangelism Committee in a congregation or synod might use this book together. It could be a seminary textbook. It is written to be used by people in many church bodies who face the same question of the education evangelism connection. It could be used by a cluster of congregations, all of one denomination or ecumenically. Likewise it could serve conference, district, synodical, or church-wide groups. It would be helpful for leaders in various educational arms of the church from pre-school to colleges as they think through their evangelizing mission of education.

Questions for Reflection and Conversation. At the end of each chapter are open-ended questions. These are designed for the individual reader and for group conversation. Thus the "study guide" is *within* the book. The questions are intended to help people appreciate their current educational and evangelizing ministries and to stretch and challenge them more deeply educationally and theologically for their particular ministry callings.

Parish Strategies. At the end of each chapter, parish strategies provide specific, concrete actions that faith communities can do in their own parish neighborhoods and beyond. Each of these arises from the specific content of the chapter. Faith communities will have ideas of their own that may well go way behind the suggestions presented here. The goal is to move from conversation to action.

Appreciation

The authors of this book wish to thank Bill Huff, Gloria Bengtson and Timothy Larson of Augsburg Fortress for their skills, encouragement, and support in bringing this book to publication. At Wartburg Seminary, Sandra Burroughs, student assistant to Norma Cook Everist, provided collegial insight as well as astute technical skills in working with chapters. She also prepared the Bibliography and the Index. Mary McDermott, faculty secretary, provided invaluable help in preparation of the manuscript. Each of the authors extends appreciation to their respective seminary communities, faculty colleagues, staff, and especially to the students who are becoming leaders in their commitment to education and evangelism.

PART ONE

EMBRACING THE QUESTIONS

1. EDUCATION AND EVANGELISM: IS THE CONNECTION ESSENTIAL?

Diane J. Hymans

Education and evangelism have been linked ever since Jesus charged the twelve to go make disciples, baptize them, and "[teach] them to obey everything I have commanded you . . ." (Matt. 28:19-20, italics mine). Go, make disciples, baptize, and teach. The text probably does not mean that things should always be done in that order, but it does suggest that, in relation to the proclamation of the gospel—or we could say evangelism—making disciples, baptizing, and teaching are closely connected. To say that evangelism and teaching—or education—are connected, however, is not to say that they are the same thing. [1]

Both words—*evangelism* and *education*—suggest a variety of meanings. One source reports that there have been over three hundred definitions of the concept "evangelize" offered in print. [2] Evangelism often conjures up images of street-corner preachers, altar calls, or even knocking on doors to invite people to church. These forms of evangelism make many people uncomfortable. But, there is another, more holistic way to think about the matter. The authors of the book *The Evangelizing Church: A Lutheran Contribution* [3] argue that evangelizing is central to the heart of the church's life and ministry. It occurs through the spoken Word, through the sacraments, and in the life of the Christian community. It is making the gospel known in both the church and the world. And rather than being the task of the clergy alone, evangelizing is integral to the baptismal vocation of all Christians. [4] These authors prefer the word "evangelizing" to "evangelism," because the meaning of the latter is too often limited to matters of program and method—for example, knocking on doors as a congregation's sole concept of evangelism. Evangelizing, in this sense, lies at the heart of what the church is. That is the understanding that we will work with here.

If this is what we mean by evangelism, then, what is the connection with education?

What Do We Mean by Education?

The word *education* is not very popular in church circles these days. "I don't like to talk in terms of 'education,'" I heard someone say not too long ago. "It's just about head stuff. Faith is more about the heart." Or, for another example, in a recent book exploring what kind of church might be needed in the twenty-first century, the author takes issue with what he calls the "education formation" model. Instead, he chooses to use the term *spiritual formation*, by which he means "how people become Christian and live in faith."[5] Education, the book argues, is too concerned with right belief, or the basics of the faith. The author suggests that spiritual formation is a more holistic way of helping people integrate faith into all areas of their lives.[6]

Spiritual formation is just one term that people are substituting for *Christian education*. Other descriptions include faith formation, faith nurture, discipleship, and lifelong learning. A person I talked with not long ago suggested that we replace "education" with "teaching and learning," because the former carries too many negative connotations.

What is the primary concern here? The widely reported decline in membership in mainline churches may be part of the problem. As people look at the decreasing numbers, they are asking questions. Why do so many people seem to be dropping out of church, especially our younger members? Where are they going? Have we been doing a good job of passing on the faith to our children in a way that invites them to understand and experience what it really means in our lives and theirs? These are real and complex questions. Perhaps because children and youth are too often seen as the primary participants in programs of Christian education—though adults surely belong there as well—those very programs are easy targets for blame as we search for answers.

Others argue that education does not seem to be doing the job it is intended to do. Why is it, they ask, that so many people do not know the stories of the Bible or are unable to articulate the basic tenets of the faith and what they mean for their lives, even after years of attending Sunday school? Does the church need something other than education to solve this problem? Or does the answer lie elsewhere?

Perhaps another reason that the notion of education carries negative connotations for many people is that they equate education with schooling. Some may be reminded of negative experiences from their own school days, experiences that made them uncomfortable, or were even hurtful. In American culture today, education often is not seen in a positive light. The public perception fed by the media, whether accurate or not, is that our schools are failing. Many people simply do not like school or do not trust schools to do the job of educating children. Because Christian education has often taken the form of schooling, it may be included in the general sense of unhappiness that some people feel toward schools.[7]

For whatever reason, many are looking for other language to use to talk about the teaching ministry of the church. All of the alternative words and concepts for Christian education that have been proposed are good ones, and they each have some relation to education. Many people express concern for the matter of growing in faith or in the life of faith, and for helping people integrate faith and life. And most want to emphasize that faith is about more than the ability to articulate beliefs, or simply "head knowledge," as some would say. It is also a matter of the heart and hand. Several of the alternative concepts suggested are broader than education. *Formation, nurture,* and *discipleship* may fall into this category. *Teaching and learning* simply name the primary activities of education. And *lifelong learning* is a reminder that education in faith is intended for more than children and youth. It should continue throughout the lifespan. Let us look at a few of these terms in more depth.

Formation—or sometimes *spiritual formation* or *faith formation*—is a popular term right now. It is often understood to refer to the entirety of an individual's experience in a particular community that shapes one's way of life. Formation involves a person's interactions with the relationships, practices, narratives, and norms that incorporate the identity of a community.[8] Formation is about the process of becoming a thinking, feeling, and acting person. If we take the congregation as one example of such a formative community, we could say that the formation of individuals into a life of faith occurs through all of the ways in which they participate in the faith community. Persons are shaped through the ways that the identity of a particular congregation is expressed in its worship, fellowship, mission, and service opportunities, as well as those experiences that are specifically educational, there is a great deal of interest in the role that parents play in the faith formation of their children. The family is obviously another formative community, but its role in faith formation is played out in relation to the larger context of the faith community.

Education is certainly formative, and should be. And Christian educators would do well to pay attention to the unique formative aspects of their work and their relationship to the life of the larger faith community. Formation is a necessary component in growth in the life of faith. It is an inevitable outcome of being with and interacting with individuals in their never-ending process of becoming Christian. But, although education is almost always an integral part of the formative process, it has a particular role to play. Formation is a larger concept. We should note, also, that formation may carry negative overtones. The faith community must always ask itself a number of important questions: Who is doing the forming? By what authority? Is it coercive? Does the individual being formed understand what is happening? Where is the gospel present? Most of our formative experiences in the church would not be seen in this negative light, but the possibility is there.

The concept *nurture* is another term that has broader connotations than "education." It often suggests metaphors of planting seeds and helping to grow strong healthy plants. In relation to Christian education, it usually refers to the idea of tending carefully to people's growth in the life of faith. The use of the term *nurture* in connection with Christian education may have originated in the nineteenth century with Horace Bushnell who argued, "That the child is to grow up a Christian, and never know himself as being otherwise."[9] Bushnell was reacting to the revivalist mentality, so popular in his day, that held that baptized children needed a dramatic conversion experience at some point in life before they could be fully admitted to membership in the church and to the Lord's table. Bushnell's strong emphasis on the role of parents in nurturing the faith of the child is an idea that is again finding a place in educational circles in the church.

Since Bushnell's day, it is also not uncommon to hear all that we do in Christian education referred to as nurture. This term is often used in a way similar to formation in that the intent is that faith is nurtured—or grows—through all of our experiences in the life of the faith community and through the efforts of parents at home. The concept *nurture* offers strong images of love and care that are necessary to growing and understanding faith. In that sense, it does not carry the coercive connotation that can be associated with formation. Although it, too, is a broader concept than education, its meaning should not be lost on those concerned about education in the church. The love and care at the heart of the gospel must certainly find expression in the educational process in the faith community.

The popularity of the term *discipleship* in relation to the ministry of education may derive from the fact that its meaning is so clearly related to learning. The Greek word for disciple, *mathetes,* means "learner." It suggests an apprentice or pupil related to a particular teacher or movement. Disciples sit at the feet of the master.[10] And, of course, the master from whom we in the church learn is Jesus. Discipleship suggests that we are learning the "way" of the one whom we follow. Disciples are learners *and* followers. Those who prefer this term may do so because of its emphasis on the *life* of discipleship. It reminds us that learning about the faith involves more than ideas. It is also concerned with how we live.

Christian educators should not ignore any of these terms or their connotations when they consider their ministry. *Formation* reminds us that we must attend to the role of the entire faith community as we plan for teaching and learning. *Nurture* lifts up the significance of caring concern in the educational process. And *discipleship* calls attention to learning and following the way of the One who calls us. Education is a part of each of these concepts and each has a role to play in educational ministry. But education itself has something unique to offer the church. That is why we need to look at this specific ministry: Jesus told his disciples to go and teach, and teaching is at the heart of education.

The reason that so many are looking for other names to describe the church's teaching ministry may have to do, not so much with the activity of education itself, but with how we understand this term and what we expect education to do. What are we talking about when we refer to the church's ministry of education? What do we hope it will do for the faith community and for individual Christians?

What Is the Educational Ministry of the Church?

There are probably as many definitions for *education* as there are for *evangelism*. For some people, education is all of our life's experience. They would say that we are learning all the time; that everything we do is educational. In relation to Christian education, the argument is, simply, that by being part of the faith community and experiencing its life and practices, people are being educated in faith. The experience of being in community together is inherently educational.[11]

Others, as mentioned earlier, understand education in terms of schooling. If some define everything we do as education, those who understand education as schooling would confine it to structured learning experiences with designated teachers, usually taking place in clearly defined classrooms, and involving lesson plans, textbooks, and learning activities.

There is truth in both of these ways of understanding education, though each of them has problems as well. While we do learn from all of our experiences, there is always the possibility that we may misunderstand, or draw the wrong conclusion. Consequently, I would suggest that education has an element of intentionality about it. We plan for it and expect that something significant will happen to learners as a result of our plans. We hope for definite learning outcomes, though those outcomes can never be guaranteed. Nor is the learning limited to what we have planned. Often in the process, much more occurs than we had ever intended or hoped.

The life experience of our students may well become part of our intentional educational process. Our experience in all of life, including the life of faith, is a rich, educational resource. Our plans may call for learners to reflect on their experience in order to learn from it. But, in the educational process, learning is most effective when it results from interaction with others with whom we can test our ideas and receive the benefit of their experience and wisdom in return. Education is not only intentional, it is also relational. It occurs in the presence of and in interaction with others. In the church, the community of faith becomes the context for our learning and becomes a partner in the process. There we bring the scriptures and the historical faith tradition into the conversation as well. We engage in education when we are in intentional conversation in relationship with other teachers and learners about our experience as the people of God in light of the church's tradition.

That reflection may occur in classrooms, but it is not limited to that context. We need to distinguish between education and schooling. Although education is intentional, and we certainly hope that it is occurring in all of our schools, including Sunday schools, it is important to remind ourselves that education is not identical to schooling. For approximately the last two hundred years, the church has relied on Sunday school as its primary model for education in faith. However, education can happen through conversation anywhere— in classrooms and living rooms, in committee meetings and choir rehearsals, at camps or retreats, and even in the car on the way to the retreat. In fact, in the church, education *must* take place in many different contexts. The Sunday school, though still playing a vital role in the church's educational ministry, cannot do the job alone. The task is too big and too complex in today's world. We need a larger understanding of educational ministry, one that recognizes that education in the church is occurring wherever and whenever people of faith are intentionally engaged in conversation about the church's tradition in relation to their own experience.

Education in the church and elsewhere is fundamentally about helping people understand. It is a response to the question, "What does this mean?" What does it mean to be a Christian? To be a follower of Jesus? To live one's faith in all of life? That kind of understanding is deep and multifaceted. It goes beyond the simply cognitive, or "head knowledge." It is personal and interpersonal. It is shaped by our emotions, and it reshapes them in return. Understanding is more than simply knowing, although it involves knowledge. It moves from the facts themselves to what those facts mean. It does not stop at what we believe, but asks why we believe what we do and what is the significance of our beliefs.

Understanding involves being able to use what we know creatively and flexibly in a variety of contexts and situations. In relation to faith, it involves integrating belief into our practice of the faith so that belief and practice are consistent with each other—what we often refer to as applying faith to life. Sometimes understanding requires that we step outside of ourselves in order to get a wider perspective on our beliefs or ideas, to test our own point of view and assumptions against those of others. At other times, we must walk in the shoes of the other in an attempt to feel as they might feel or see as they might see. Here, understanding calls for empathy. Understanding requires that we involve all of our selves. This kind of understanding is *mindful* faith, or to put it another way, loving God with our minds.[12] But, it is not just about head knowledge. As one lay theologian stated, "If I love Jesus, I want to learn as much as I can about him. Book-larnin' (*sic*) is not pitted against spirituality, or a substitute for it, but is a natural tendency of the heart."[13]

Understanding takes many forms. Understanding the doctrine of justification is a different matter from understanding Handel's *Messiah*. The process of understanding another person is not the same thing as understanding how to pray. What does it mean to understand God? Understanding does not happen all at once; it truly is lifelong. As the writer to the Corinthians suggests, in matters of faith, we will not fully understand until we "see face to face" (1 Cor. 13: 12-13).

There are times when we discover that we have misunderstood something that we thought we knew well. Understanding may occasionally involve a change of mind or even a change of heart. The path to understanding may lie in our willingness to admit our lack of understanding. It often requires that we be open to ideas and to persons who represent viewpoints that differ from our own. "We should be teachable, honest, [having] integrity. Knowledge puffs up, but we should recognize the limits of our knowledge and not think that we have it all figured out."[14] Understanding, in this sense, is a form of conversion. It is a continuing process of learning and re-learning in relation to the journey of faith.[15]

This concept of education is more a process than a program. It is an ongoing conversation among teachers and learners around a subject in which each has a role to play. The goal is to lead toward broader and deeper comprehension and appropriation by the learner—and also by the teacher—in search of understanding. In the process, even the subject matter might be changed, as teachers and learners discover new ways to make sense of it in light of their own context and experience.[16]

Education and Faith

I believe that we need to maintain the language of education to name and describe what is an essential ministry in the church. Education clearly has something to do with faith. But what is the nature of that relationship. Is faith learned? If so, how? If not, what role does education play in relation to faith? And if education is primarily about understanding, what is it that we need to understand?

The word *faith* is another concept that resists simple definition. It is often said that everyone has faith of some kind. All believe in something and place trust somewhere—in wealth, family, job, country, whatever. Faith, in this sense, is essentially a human activity. But, from the Christian perspective, faith begins with God who calls us into relationship. Because of human sin, that relationship is possible only because God has taken the initiative to reach out to us by making God's self known through Jesus the Christ. Through the life, death, and resurrection of Jesus, we discover who God is and who God is calling us to be. Faith is a response to God's initiative. Faith is the recognition and acceptance of the grace that is offered to us by God, which results in a desire to live a unique way of life based on gratitude, trust, and commitment. Faith itself is not something "learned." It is a gift that we receive with joy and thanksgiving.

Education is a response to the question, "What does this mean?" Education results from the desire to understand God and to comprehend what it means to live the life of faith to which God is calling us. Christian educator, Sara Little writes in her book, *To Set One's Heart: Belief and Teaching in the Church*, that the questioning of meaning is at the heart of being human: "We need to be more deliberate in our approach to helping persons claim the Christian inheritance in such a way that they can come to know who they are and why they are."[17] The ELCA Task Force on Education (see chapter 12) has said that the Church's specific ministry in education is to instruct and form faithful and wise disciples to live out their baptismal vocation in the Church and world. The answer to *who* we are is: we are disciples of Jesus Christ. The answer to *why* we are is: to live out our baptismal vocation in the church and also in the world. Who we are—our identity—and why we are—our vocation—provide a focus for evangelizing and a purpose for education in the church. The search to understand what these questions mean and how they are to be answered brings us to the heart of the Christian faith and is the essence of educational ministry.

Content, Beliefs, and Practices

Where do we go in our search to understand these matters? We go to the church's tradition. We study the scriptures; we consider how the church has answered our questions through its history; we examine our confessional documents; we engage our own experience in conversation with all of these resources. Our faith has a content that is found in the story told in the scriptures and the church's teachings through the ages. That content offers us a language in the form of beliefs and practices that allows us to name and describe the life of faith.

Christian education is often criticized for focusing too much on teaching beliefs or doctrine without paying attention to what they mean in our daily lives. The argument is that too much attention is paid to sterile content and not enough to living faith. Although there may be some truth to that accusation, the corrective to the problem is not to ignore content altogether. Knowing what we believe is not all there is to faith, but a faith without knowledge of belief and meaning is empty and easily misguided.

Sara Little offers a holistic understanding of belief and its relation to faith, defining belief generally as "*an idea held (thought and experienced) to be true.*"[18] We hold beliefs about many things, and those beliefs are derived from many sources and experiences. But, *Christian* beliefs are rooted in the Christian tradition. They have to do with how we understand ourselves and our world in relation to the God we know in Jesus Christ. For Little, faith and belief are not identical. Faith is always the primary category. "Faith *is* a trust, loyalty, confidence, but it is more than a 'feeling.' It is a trust qualified by the One who is trusted. It is, in fact, a gift from that One who reveals himself."[19]

Belief becomes the path by which we appropriate, at deeper and deeper levels, what our faith means as we explore our faith tradition in light of our own experiences. Belief grows out of faith and, in turn, reshapes it. Believing is not just thinking, though thought is clearly involved. Belief involves not only our minds, but also our emotions, our actions, and our wills. Beliefs are not just ideas that we hold, but ideas that we *are*. Little lifts up the word *credo*, which is usually translated as "I believe." Its literal meaning is "I set my heart." It is a move from "believing that" to "believing in." [20] That is the kind of belief that transforms lives and gives meaning and direction to faith. Formation of that kind of belief is the reason for teaching in the church.

More recently, attention has been drawn to another dimension of the faith—its practices, the things that Christians do that shape a way of life. There are a variety of formal definitions for "practice." The one first offered by Dorothy Bass and Craig Dykstra is: "Christian practices are things Christian people do together over time in response to and in the light of God's active presence for the life of the world."[21] There are also multiple lists of Christian practices, which include such things as worshipping, praying, offering hospitality, discernment, healing, keeping Sabbath, giving testimony, practicing justice, forgiving one another, and shaping community.[22] These practices can be traced back to the beginnings of the church. They are entangled in the activities of everyday human life. The doing of them connects us to God and to each other. They must be learned, which means that they have a significant place in the church's educational ministry.

Belief and practice are not two entirely separate categories of faith. Rather, they are inextricably linked to one another. Though this linkage is complex and sometimes flawed (that is to say, our practices do not always truly reflect what we believe, and what we profess is not always lived out in our practice), we are still able to say that our practices shape what we believe, and our beliefs, in turn, shape our practices.[23] Just as the understanding takes a lifetime of education, so surely does integration of faith and practice. Education is, in part, a process of discerning truth. It is a continual process of asking whether the beliefs we confess truly reflect the God whom we know in Jesus Christ and whether our practices are an authentic living out of that faith. In all that we say and do, are we being faithful people? The effort to understand the meaning of our beliefs and the form of our practices should help us claim our identities and live out our vocations in response to God's call.

An educational process that focuses on belief and practice must be situated in the center of the community of faith, because that is their source. The act of worship, for example, cannot be fully understood without actually participating in the worshipping life of a faith community. At the same time, there are many aspects of worship that we cannot comprehend without someone teaching us about them—such things as what do the particular elements of the liturgy mean and, why are those elements arranged in the order that they are? In today's entertainment culture, people often have trouble understanding what religious worship is and what role they play; that they are the actors and not the audience, and that worship is about God, not just about themselves. This knowledge is not necessarily intuitive. Worship consists of both belief and practice. We cannot fully understand either dimension without both intentional teaching and experiencing worship in community.

One final word on education and faith: Education is not just about receiving the faith tradition; it is also about questioning it and adapting it in response to new situations and contexts. Our teaching must incorporate elements of both continuity and change. Education in the church serves both to initiate persons into the tradition and to help persons adapt that tradition to changing social and historical contexts. Initiation may apply especially to children and to newcomers to the faith, perhaps even to those who are not yet ready to commit to it. In *Christianity for the Rest of Us*, Diana Butler Bass tells of congregations who welcome into their study groups "doubting Thomases"—people who are not yet sure about the faith, but who are interested enough to ask probing questions. Bass suggests that, too often, churches discourage those questions by offering easy answers too quickly before people have had a chance to articulate their doubts and questions and to wrestle with the complexities of relating faith to the dilemmas they face in their everyday lives.[24] Could the practice of making room for questioning in educational contexts in the church be a form of evangelizing?

The challenge of understanding what our faith means in a rapidly changing world calls for the use of playful imagination in an educational process where continuity with the faith tradition is balanced by the possibility of change. As we experience new realities in our world and in our personal lives—cultural and ethnic diversity in our neighborhoods, a global economy, terrorism and war, a new baby, job loss, the death of a friend, marriage, divorce, and more—we struggle to figure out how our beliefs and practices can meet the new challenges that are presented. The Christian faith has never been a fixed tradition. After Jesus left the disciples, they had to figure out what to do next, and the church was born. Martin Luther questioned the practices of the church in his day, and the result was the Protestant Reformation. Change for us may not be as dramatic or as cataclysmic, but it is a continuing reality.

We are called to engage our imaginations in playful ways to try out new possibilities of understanding and practicing faith. According to one educator, "Imagination is the capacity to think of things as possibly being so."[25] In a world that often seems devoid of faith or in which the church is seen as irrelevant, the need for imagination to believe in and understand a God of grace may be absolutely necessary. An understanding of authentic discipleship in this consumer-oriented, media-saturated culture calls for an active imagination to envision another way of living in relation to each other and to God. We need to imagine that our faith just might possibly be true and to translate what we discover about our faith in scripture and the church's tradition into a living reality in the contemporary world.

Education and Evangelism

So what is the relationship between education and evangelizing? They are not identical. Evangelizing is making the gospel known in church and world. It is similar to proclamation understood in the broadest sense—proclamation in the form of both spoken word and lived experience. Education focuses on understanding the gospel and how it shapes who we are and the way we live our lives. Clearly, we cannot draw too a fine a distinction between these two essential ministries of the church. As people hear the gospel proclaimed, they often come to understand, in profound ways, who God is and who they are. And the gospel is made known in countless ways, both intentionally and unintentionally, in educational settings in the faith community. Clearly both are needed in the church and the world. The difference is one of focus and purpose, not importance.

Although education is not the same thing as evangelizing, it is absolutely essential to it. Education invites people to understand and claim their identity as baptized children of God and to clarify their vocation as people called by God to live lives characterized by love of God and neighbor. Education helps people articulate the meaning of the gospel for themselves, for others, and for the world. In this way, education prepares those already in the church to share the gospel. And the ministry of education provides a venue for those who are newly welcomed into the faith community to understand what it is to which they have committed their lives. For them, it offers a language of belief and practice with which to name their experience of the gospel that has been proclaimed to them and around which they can structure their lives as disciples of Christ.

"Go therefore and make disciples . . . baptizing them . . . and teaching them" (Mt. 28:19–20).

Questions for Reflection and Conversation

1. What terminology do you use to name educational ministry in your congregation? Why have you chosen it? How does the language you use shape the way you carry out your educational ministry?

2. What impact has educational ministry had on your faith? Recall places and people who were part of those education experiences.

3. How has your understanding of faith changed throughout your lifetime? How has education, in the broadest sense, played a role in that process?

Parish Strategies

1. With a group of people interested in educational ministry, talk about where education, formally and informally, is happening in your congregation, beyond the Sunday school. In what contexts is it happening, formally and informally, beyond the congregation? How can education become integrated more fully into the life of the whole church?

2. With the same group of people, or another group, if appropriate, talk about the potential of integrating a focus on beliefs and practices into your educational ministry. How could giving attention to specific practices of faith strengthen your ministry of education and help people grow in the life of faith?.

Education is not only intentional, it is also relational.

2. WHAT ARE THE THEOLOGICAL FOUNDATIONS OF CHRISTIAN EDUCATION AND EVANGELISM?

Margaret A. Krych

We sometimes are inclined to divide education and evangelism and to treat them as separate activities. Occasionally, we even pit them against one another.

"Susan, I'm on the evangelism committee."

"That's great, Joyce. I think that fits you. For myself, I'm not really into evangelism. I'm on the education committee—education is much more my thing."

Such a dichotomy is not only detrimental to the life of the church, but is actually theologically wrong. Education and evangelism belong together. They are two sides of one coin.

A Vocation to Share the Good News

Consider the Reformation. One is hard pressed to know whether it was an effort in re-evangelization (bringing the gospel to those already baptized, who did not truly know the good news) or an effort in education. Martin Luther's horror at the state of the congregations during the visitation of 1528–1529 was one of the primary motivations for writing the *Small Catechism*: "The deplorable, wretched deprivation that I recently encountered while I was a visitor has constrained and compelled me to prepare this catechism. . . . The ordinary person, especially in the villages, knows absolutely nothing about the Christian faith, and unfortunately many pastors are completely unskilled and incompetent teachers. Yet supposedly they all bear the name Christian, are baptized, and receive the holy sacrament, even though they do not know the Lord's Prayer, the Creed, or the Ten Commandments."[1] In other words, the people did not know the gospel and needed to hear it. This process of re-evangelization was actually an educational campaign. Or, one might equally say, this educational program was an important evangelistic tool in the sixteenth century.

Early church catecheses included both teaching and evangelizing, preparing those coming into the Christian faith so that they were ready for baptism, for incorporation into the community called Church. In many congregations today, evangelism and education go hand in hand in preparing previously unchurched adults for baptism.

Our call in baptism as members of the church is, in fact, a call to the vocation of evangelist-teacher or teacher-evangelist wherever we are. Jesus said, "Go therefore and make disciples of all nations, baptizing them in the name of the Father and of the Son and of the Holy Spirit, and teaching them to obey everything that I have commanded you"(Matt. 28:20). This making of disciples, or teaching, may be overseas, in a local community, in a congregation, or in our own family. The function is the same, whether it is communicating the gospel for the first time to someone who has never heard it, reminding those who know it vaguely and clarifying their understanding, or speaking it to those who know it well, but need daily to hear again the comfort for their consciences. Seen from one point of view, it is evangelizing. Seen from another, it is teaching.

Some denominations witness the unity of evangelism and education by putting the two under the same departmental structure heading in the national structure. (The Evangelical Lutheran Church in America is one such body that follows this wise practice in the United States.) Other denominations may have them in separate structures, but endeavor to keep them connected. Whatever the structure, the task of keeping them linked is ongoing and essential.

The Good News We Share

Christians are called to share the good news—the gospel message that in Christ God has acted decisively to deal with sin so that, through faith, we may receive God's merciful forgiveness. This message has two sides that must not be confused, yet must always be held together. One side is a word of judgment, a word that condemns all of our human ambitions and pretenses and reveals that we human beings stand before God as rebellious, disobedient, and pretentious to the point of setting ourselves as the objects of our trust and worship rather than God. This is a word that tells of our human needs. We call this side of the message, the law. Or, to use Paul Tillich's term, it can be called the "question"[2]—really, the deep questions which are part of our human existence from the very beginning.

The other side of the message is the incredibly good news that God loves us and accepts us through Christ in spite of our sin, guilt, self-centeredness, and rebellion. God is merciful and acts graciously toward us, even though we do not deserve it. Through Christ's obedience and suffering, we are granted forgiveness and new life. This answer comes to us from God. It is not something that we have devised, but a Word from God to us. Through this Word, God the Spirit calls forth faith in us. It is all God's work; and, it is all due to God's love for us. This good news is the gospel. Or, to use Paul Tillich's term, it is the "answer" that God provides to our deepest human questions and needs. We must hold together law and gospel (or, correlate question and answer) without confusing the one with the other, and we must speak of them clearly and in a way that makes sense to the hearer. The answer to the deepest human questions is Jesus Christ—but we must relate that answer to the way the human questions are formulated or experienced by persons in particular contexts (see chapter 11). Otherwise, our communication will be perceived as irrelevant or meaningless.

Every Christian is called to share this twofold message. The deep questions of estrangement from God are experienced by children, youth, and adults in every facet of their lives. Tillich, for example, examines how alienation is experienced in our reason, our sense of finitude, our relationships, our life experiences, and world history.[3] The teacher-evangelist's task is to relate the answer of God in Jesus Christ to those human experiences of ambiguity and guilt. In the process, the teacher-evangelist helps hearers begin to shape their own questions evermore clearly so that God's answer may truly be perceived as precisely the answer that each person needs to hear.[4]

The scriptures give us the parameters of the message we are to communicate. It is our task to translate the scriptural message from the formulations and language of 2000 years ago into terms that make sense in our contemporary world and in individual lives today. This is the careful and sometimes tricky task of the evangelist and the educator.

Such sharing of the good news includes not just proclaiming the message of forgiveness but also what theologians term *apologetics*, that is, commending the faith, giving a reason for believing, interpreting misunderstandings, and clearing away misconceptions. It includes not only knowing the scriptures, but also being cognizant of questions which nonbelievers may ask and of the ways in which answers may be perceived as appropriate, relevant, and respectful.

Evangelization and education belong together theologically and practically. We cannot speak the gospel if we do not know what it is. Many Christians do not feel confident as communicators. The pastor of a congregation in Pennsylvania announced that there would be a new outreach to the community; people would go from door to door to talk about their faith. The members froze with fear. One after another said, "But what if people ask questions? I don't know how to answer questions." "How can I tell them my faith? I sort of know it, but not well enough to discuss it with anybody."

The pastor wisely realized that before any sharing of the message could take place, a new adult-education initiative was necessary. A number of classes were started with the purpose of clarifying the basics of the faith. These gave adults the opportunity to talk about their faith and the message of the Scriptures. Actually hearing their own voices expressing their faith was a novel experience for many. After a year of education, the witnessing program finally got underway with some exciting results. As one member put it, "I don't know everything by any means, but I've learned enough to feel comfortable sharing my faith, and I feel confident enough to say when I don't have an answer and to promise I will find out and get back to the person. So now I'm ready to go door-knocking."

The gospel is not simply a message for others. The evangelist and the educator are themselves also addressed by the gospel. Every baptized Christian daily returns to the word of judgment and forgiveness, of law and gospel, to hear again the good news of God's merciful acceptance of us in spite of the fact that we are unacceptable—what Paul calls justification by grace through faith. A professor of Bible, Martin Luther nevertheless said of himself, "I must still read and study the catechism daily, and yet I cannot master it as I wish, but must remain a child and pupil of the catechism—and I also do so gladly."[5] His advice to all pastors was, "It is highly profitable and fruitful to read [the catechism] daily and to make it the subject of meditation and conversation. In such reading, conversation and meditation the Holy Spirit is present and bestows ever new and greater light and devotion, so that it tastes better and better."[6]

In Baptism, we first participated in the death and resurrection of Christ for the forgiveness of our sin. God's gracious Word comes to us again every day, acting upon us, killing our sinful selves, and raising us to new life. This is all God's doing—not our best efforts—but God's free grace that makes us and keeps us children of God. As we return daily to our baptism, we thank God that we were claimed by grace in the death and resurrection of Jesus Christ for our salvation before we ever knew about it and even before we were born. That gracious action of God drives us out to share the good news with others.

Evangelists and teachers need each other and, above all, need the community of the church gathered around Word and Sacraments, through which God the Holy Spirit creates faith and gives to us the promise of forgiveness of sin over and over again. In teaching and evangelizing, we remember that we are incorporated by baptism, not only into a congregation and denomination, but into the one, holy, catholic, and apostolic church. The gospel cuts across denominational and national barriers. Therefore, in communicating the gospel to others, we do so not from a narrow sectarian point of view, but in a way that speaks to persons from all walks of life and traditions.

Teaching and evangelizing usually use words. But equally necessary and important is the way we live and serve others as we engage in the world. People look at our actions and compare them to our words. Much careful teaching and earnest evangelizing have been undercut when the deeds of the communicators have denied their words.

Functions of the Church

Why do evangelizing and teaching belong so closely together? Paul Tillich clearly articulates the connection between the two on the basis of Christ and the Church. He holds that, in confessing Jesus as the Christ, the universality of the community of believers throughout the world and throughout history is implied and this, in turn, demands the "expansion functions" of the Church.[7] The good news of Jesus Christ is for all people of all ages of all times and places. Evangelizing and education are two sides of one coin and are as old as Jesus sending the disciples, two by two. Tillich highlights three expansion functions: missions, education, and evangelism.

Missions: "The first function of expansion, historically and systematically," Tillich explains, "is missions. . . . Whenever active members of the church encounter those outside the church, they are missionaries of the church, voluntarily or involuntarily. Their very being is missionary."[8] So, we may correctly speak of missions as sharing with others who have never heard the gospel—in all the world and also here in North America, where many unchurched persons live as our neighbors in our communities.

The message of the church is not abstract. "It is always embodied in a particular culture."[9] The Holy Spirit can use traditional cultural categories to speak of that which concerns us ultimately. So we go to other cultures to share the good news. Or we communicate with those from different subcultures within our own broad culture. There is always the danger of imposing our own culture or subculture on others in the name of Christ. We must recognize what is from our culture and be self-critical and honest about it. We are not (or should not be) in the business of bringing our own culture to dominate others, but rather, we are seeking to understand the others' cultures and to bring the gospel in terms of those cultures.

Communication of the gospel to those who have never heard it is a calling, a vocation of all Christians given in baptism. Our priesthood in daily life includes proclaiming the Word, interceding for others, and bearing the others' burdens for Christ's sake. This vocation is expressed in the various settings in our daily life—home, family, congregation, wider church, workplace or school, leisure, volunteer organizations, and so on. In these settings, the word of judgment and mercy may be spoken by Christians one-on-one or to groups or institutions. Wherever Christians are, justification by grace through faith calls them to speak and to work for reconciliation, justice, love, peace, and truth; to hear confession and to speak of forgiveness; and to give caring service attentive to the neighbors' needs.

Some persons on behalf of the Church will travel to far-off places to share the good news with those who have never heard it. Some will support and pray for indigenous churches to grow and flourish. Some of those from far-off places will travel to our own shores to be missionaries to the United States and Canada. Many will not travel far at all, but will stay locally witnessing to the gospel to those who do not know it and who are legion in many societies, including our own.

Education: "The second function of expansion is based on the desire of the churches to continue their life from generation to generation—the function of education."[10] Tillich says that this function started the moment the first family was received into the church and is directed to those who are baptized. Whether they are children or adults, the baptized need to hear—in terms appropriate to their age-level—the word of law and gospel, of judgment and forgiveness, of the good news of God's merciful acceptance of us in spite of the fact that we are unacceptable. Justification by grace through faith lies at the heart of Christian education.

An important ministry of the Word is that which we speak to one another in families. Good parenting includes teaching the good news to our offspring. As the earliest Christian educators for the child, parents provide foundational stability, trust, love, and security that is essential if the child is later to develop an understanding of God as stable, secure, loving, and trustworthy. Healthy parenting is foundational for communicating the gospel to children.

We also teach in the local congregation. We do not just communicate knowledge or correct formulations of doctrine, important as those may be. Rather, we introduce each new generation to the spiritual community, the church, into its faith and into its love.[11] Obviously, this introduction is gradual and is done in ways appropriate to the age level.[12]

Those who teach on behalf of the congregation spend many hours in training and preparation of lessons. They deserve the support of the congregation through prayer, good materials and adequate teaching supplies, and warm thanks and encouragement. Those who teach professionally and regularly on behalf of the church—pastors, religious education directors, teachers in Christian schools—particularly need the prayers and support of the church. In turn, the church has the responsibility to remind teachers that they are exercising a God-given vocation, and that teaching is a high and holy calling that requires faithfulness, preparation, training, and the Holy Spirit's constant aid. Congregations need ongoing, stimulating, and supportive teaching education, and should begin to offer such opportunities if they are not now doing so. Christian education is both an opportunity to speak the Word and a means of serving and loving the neighbors, their students, in the congregational setting.

Baptism witnesses to a gospel that cuts across denominational and national barriers. It is a sign of Christian unity. We have been incorporated, not only into a congregation and denomination, but into the one, holy, catholic, and apostolic church. Baptism brings us into a worldwide, historical community that is called to be trustworthy and faithful. Sometimes teachers may forget the primary function of incorporation into the universal church and focus, instead, on incorporating students into a particular congregation or denomination. But incorporation into the church catholic, the whole universal Body of Christ, demands that we must first emphasize the breadth of the church throughout the centuries and today, focusing more on what the various branches of the church have in common through the Scriptures, rather than on differences that divide. This does not mean that we should ignore points of difference, but that we should put differences in the context of Christ's one universal Body.

Of course, as sinful beings, our teaching is shot through and through with selfishness and narrow vision. Yet, we pray that the power of the Holy Spirit will work through us, helping us to overcome our sinful tendencies and to truly speak a word that brings mercy and comfort to those whom we teach. Effective communication of the gospel to the next generation is possible only by the power of the presence of God, the Holy Spirit.[13]

Is all education consonant with evangelizing? There will be occasions in Christian education when what we teach will be broader than the law-gospel message. Factual material, at first glance, does not seem to fall into a question-answer pattern, for example, teaching the names of the books of the Bible or the geography of Israel. However, we must consider why we might teach such material at all. Normally, it is as background to the central task of communicating the gospel. One could make a similar case for teaching about culture and traditions before evangelizing so that the gospel can be clearly expressed in mission settings. These serve the gospel as necessary preparation for the communication of the news of Jesus Christ.

How about education in the broadest terms? At the time of the Reformation, Martin Luther had remarkable insight into the function of education. He saw education as much more than just teaching the Bible. In fact, he saw that education prepares us in two spheres, or realms, that serve God and of which God is the sovereign ruler. On the one hand is the sphere of creation in which God has given the law to serve humankind and maintain justice, peace, and order in the world and in society. In that realm are many opportunities to serve God in the arenas of daily life in families, work, church, community, and so on. Preparation for such service through good schooling is essential for the well-being of society and is eminently pleasing to God.[14] On the other hand is the realm of redemption and grace in which persons need to hear the message of the Scriptures, the good news of the gospel of Jesus Christ. That message also must be taught with clarity for the sake of all, since Jesus died for all. Such education is necessary to raise up a generation that will continue the teaching and preaching of the gospel in all of our roles and relationships within the church and in daily life.[15]

Both forms of education are necessary so that Christians can truly serve God and the neighbor in the particular stations of their life. Luther would not have understood the person who says, "I believe that education in the Bible is important, but I don't really care about education in secular subjects." Nor would he have understood the person who says, "I like to share the gospel, but I really don't like teaching my children about God," or, "I like teaching, but don't ask me to be an evangelist."

Evangelizing: The third function of expansion, says Tillich, is evangelistic, which is directed toward the church's estranged or indifferent members—those who are either inactive or actively hostile to the church.[16] In today's society, many persons have some family or cultural Christian background.[17] They are nonchurchgoers or even the second generation of nonchurchgoers. These are not the persons who faithfully practice another religion. The United States and Canada are religiously plural nations. There are many persons in these societies not affiliated with a church who still have some vestiges of Christianity. They may attend weddings and funerals and perhaps the occasional Easter or Christmas service. They may be or have been affiliated with a youth group or adult activity. But they are not active in faith or worship. They may be called "unchurched" or "dechurched."

Tillich says there are two activities involved in reaching out to these estranged persons: practical apologetics and evangelistic preaching.[18] Practical apologetics is the silent witness of the community of faith and love that convinces even those not convinced by argument. Yet persuasive argument is also necessary, of course, when the occasion arises. Evangelistic preaching is persuasive and is effective by the power of the Holy Spirit.[19] But it is effective only when persons are present to hear the preaching! Much more likely in today's society, evangelistic outreach will be the word and witness of the individual believer who is the neighbor, the tennis partner, the reading coach, the carpool driver. These are the persons who speak the gospel one-on-one to those with whom they come into daily contact. They witness to the value of Christ and the church in their lives. They offer the invitation to "come to church with me—I'll pick you up."

Sometimes people not belonging to a church send their children to Sunday schools and vacation Bible schools or voluntarily join an adult class whose topic interests them. Or they appreciate a community-service project organized by the church. Perhaps in times of grief or trauma, they seek a worship service to find some hope and meaning. Congregations ready to evangelize are attuned to visitors, warmly welcoming, and nonjudgemental, with sermons that are readily understood and with teachers who fill in gaps of information smoothly without putting visitors on the spot. A wide range of adult and youth classes allows for some courses to focus on the basics where the newcomer feels at home.

Helpful Points in Communicating the Gospel

We have said that we are engaged in the same task of correlating the universal human questions with the answers of the gospel, but with different audiences in mind. The following points will aid us in our task.

Participation:[20] The human questions are experienced differently in every time and place, and therefore the answers must also be expressed in appropriate ways. In the case of missions, there are a variety of cultures and traditions that are different from one's own. In educating children, we must take into account the qualitative differences in the way children think from the way that adults (parents and teachers) think—preoperational and concrete thinking require communication in particular ways. In dealing with teenagers, communicating the gospel must take into account the changing and surprising physical, social, and emotional situation of adolescence and the new world of responsibility, identity, and insecurity, together with the youth subculture of music, friends, and even language.

How can we know every possible situation? How can we communicate the gospel to everybody? Fortunately, none of us has to speak to every person in every time and every place. For the mission field or educational setting entrusted to us, we need to prepare and learn all we can about those with whom we are communicating. That means listening and learning and being willing to use words and experiences different from our own. The way we experience the gospel may be quite different from the way other people do. So we listen to their experiences of the questions. And then we must be prepared to reword our own witness in terms that make sense in our hearer's world.

Paul was the consummate "participant" in others' worlds—
To the Jews I became as a Jew, in order to win Jews. To those under the law I became as one under the law (though I myself am not under the law) so that I might win those under the

law. To those outside the law I became as one outside the law. . . so that I might win those outside the law. To the weak I became weak, so that I might win the weak. I have become all things to all people, so that I might by all means save some. I do it all for the sake of the gospel, so that I may share in its blessings. (I Cor. 9:20-23)

Truth and adaptation:[21] We must know the gospel thoroughly if we are to adapt the message to the language and traditions of others, while not distorting the gospel itself. Some who would evangelize and teach do not adapt the message, and it flies past the heads of people without anyone checking whether it was understood. Without adaptation to our hearers' lives, experiences, and categories of understanding, we lose people.

However, if we adapt the message in the wrong way, we may be in danger of losing the gospel. Examples are legion: the witness who tries not to offend people and dismisses the Trinity as so much gobbledygook; the youth director who wants so much to appeal to youth that she gives class time over to the latest music on the iPods and never gets around to the meat and challenge of the gospel; the seminarian who tries to put soteriology into contemporary terms and ends up with a classic heresy; the pastor who preaches a beautifully poetic sermon, but devotes so much time to the poetry that he never gets around to mentioning God's loving mercy so there is no word of comfort for the man with the drug addiction and the woman who is recovering from an abortion.

Remaining true to the Scriptures, yet interpreting the gospel in terms that make sense to persons in the supermarket checkout line or in the sports complex, is a tricky and time-consuming task that demands all the care we can muster. But every one of us is called to that task if we are to be relevant communicators of the gospel.

Similarities in the human situation:[22] No matter how different the background and experiences are, there is always something similar between the communicator of the gospel and the hearer. That point of similarity is our situation before God, our human predicament. All of us stand condemned before God. All of us have the same need to hear God's good news of mercy in Jesus Christ. This commonality gives us a positive point of entry in communicating with others. It is also a reminder that we approach others in humility. Ultimately, it is God who convicts both communicator and hearer of the truth of the Word and who gives us the whole-person response of faith as a gift.

The point of similarity in the human condition should bring comfort to the evangelizer and teacher as they seek a starting point for communication. While it may take many hours of listening and participating, the point of similarity is already there in our hearer's human existence, and we resonate with it and with them.

Not treating others as objects:[23] As sinful human beings, we are prone to treat others as objects rather than subjects. That means we are inclined to stand over against another and see her as the recipient of what I have to offer, or the learner whom I will teach. In the process we depersonalize the other as an object to be manipulated, a thing to serve our own purposes. The solution is to remember that teacher and learner, communicator and hearer, stand equally under the Word, and equally need to listen to it. Rather than, "poor ignorant person—I have the goods to show them," it is rather, "God through the Scriptures has shown me an answer to my deepest needs. You too have deep needs. Tell me what they are. We can both stand under the One who answers us all."

We are all prone to controlling others. But in communicating the gospel, there can be no superiority, even over the youngest child; no dominating, even over the weakest and most vulnerable hearer; no using people for our own ends. Because every hearer is God's own creation, every learner is someone for whom Christ died.

In communicating the gospel, there is no counting of converts, no bragging about "how many young people I have led to the Lord." It is not we who convert, nor is it we who lead anyone to the Lord—rather, the Holy Spirit draws them through the Word. We can only pray that God the Spirit will give us words and deeds to communicate clearly. As both saints and sinners, it is only in the power of the Spirit, fragmentarily, that we can truly communicate with another as subject to subject and can truly love each other. The Spirit often uses us when we are at our worst and when our efforts are most feeble.

The communicator as symbol: Tillich helps us understand what it is to be a symbol.[24] He says that symbols point beyond themselves to something else, but also participate in that to which they point. So a New Testament story about Jesus can mediate to us the power of the original event that is related in the story; it can show us who we are and who God is, and so become a means of salvation.[25] But a symbol can become demonic when it points to itself rather than to the reality it is intended to convey; it can get in the way of the message, and so be destructive.

Our task as teachers is to be transparent to the gospel, pointing beyond ourselves to Jesus Christ. We pray that we will not point to ourselves and obscure the message, but rather hope that the Spirit will give us transparency and guidance in the choice of language symbols that will truly open up the Word of God for our hearers.

Avoiding "ghetto language:" Gerhard Ebeling uses that term to warn us that Christian proclamation has largely become a private group language that we speak in the church, but which does not reflect the language of public life in the world of politics, economics, industry, science, and culture.[26] We must be able to communicate about God in terms that make sense in the public arena. We must show that the Word of God is related to our human existence in the world, that the Word of God correctly describes our human predicament and truly brings it to light. Rightly speaking of God transposes us into a new situation that brings us truth and reality through the Word, which receives its authority from Jesus. Such a word gives us freedom and a new future.

Speaking a word in the public arena may be not nearly as comfortable as speaking a word to each other in the familiar language of loved hymns, favorite songs, and prayers. But, if we are to evangelize and teach in today's secular, pluralistic world, then we must seek what Bonhoeffer called nonreligious, or worldly,[27] ways to communicate with others.

Unity of Word and Sacrament: Evangelizing is closely tied to both Word and Sacraments. The ministry of Word and Sacraments goes back to the earliest days of the Church, and all acts of ministers in teaching the gospel and leading the churches embody for the believers the church and mission that has come down from Jesus Christ himself.[28] "The secret of Jesus' real presence is this: the way he freely comes to people today is through the proclamation of his word, the celebration of the sacraments, and the life and witness of the Christian community. It is through the spoken, visible, and lived words that God's special grace in Christ is given to a hungry church and a needy world. Salvation depends on the grace of Jesus coming by special means to people and, then, being received by faith."[29]

The Word leads to faith, which in turn leads to Baptism and incorporation into the church. Evangelizing and teaching presuppose life in the people of God nourished by the Lord's Supper and preaching. Those so nourished go out by the power of the Spirit to call others to share in that same nourishing life.

Remembering the End: Contemporary theologian Wolfhart Pannenberg reminds us that all that we say and do as Christians is in the light of God's final future for the world and the Church, what we call the eschaton. God has promised to one day sum up all things and bring history to an end. In that day, the unity of humanity under God will, at last, be evident. The resurrection of Jesus is the foretaste of this end. In Jesus, we see the power of God and God's intention for the world. God's reconciling work in Christ has universal relevance and leads to mission. "Only a reference to the eschatological future of the reign of God necessarily brings the missionary dimension into the concept of the church. As the community that waits the parousia of its risen Lord, the church is called to give missionary witness to the world."[30]

So evangelists and teachers share the joyful news that the one who came and died for all is the one who will come and before whom all humans will stand. They let God's beloved know that God loves them and the future that God has in store for them, that Jesus has already taken their judgment on the cross,[31] and that they will participate in that glorious consummation of all things. The church is called so to live in unity and love that all people can see in it a microcosm of the final unity and life of love that will be God's kingdom for all humankind.

Creative love: Creative love is the link between teacher and student in education and between the communicator and the hearer in evangelization.[32] Only the Spirit of God can give us the gift of love to welcome the learner as participant and to welcome the inactive member or neighbor who is not part of a faith community as a dearly respected brother or sister. Rather than negative judgment of the other, creative love accepts the other person, as Christ accepts us. Creative love genuinely wants what is good for the other; and creative love wins the other's love in return.

Prayer and the Work of the Spirit: Both evangelizing and teaching the gospel depend totally on the work of the Holy Spirit. Therefore, both evangelist and teacher are called to prayer and faithful dependence on the Spirit. Prayer is the means by which the Holy Spirit works through us to bring others to faith through the Word. The church that undergirds us is also called to pray for its members in the calling to communicate the gospel. Such prayer belongs, not only in the local congregation, but also in the various expressions of the larger Church as it calls its members to share the good news.

Questions for Reflection and Conversation

1. Without undue pause, am I able to express the gospel to someone who asks what I believe? What might I say?

2. How seriously do we take the work of teaching and sharing the gospel in the home? What might help us do so more faithfully?

3. Do we think of ourselves as engaged in missions? What does the rapid growth of the church in other parts of the world say to us? Are we ready to welcome missionaries from other parts of the world to our country?

4. What are three ways you would recommend to your congregation to reach out to people who are not attending?

Parish Strategies

1. Develop a group that includes both teachers and evangelizers to discuss the message they have in common and to practice ways they can communicate it to those who do not attend church.

2. Visit your neighborhood with packets of information about your church, a friendly smile, and a willingness to talk about the gospel. Bring a notepad to jot down names and addresses of those who request a pastoral visit or more information or who would welcome your contacting their own pastor (of a different denomination) whom they have not seen in a long time. We can be ecumenically responsible as we seek out new people for conversation.

3. Begin an initiative in your community about a public issue that matters to your neighbors, for example, education, health, or youth. Meet on your church premises— some will come who have not put foot in a church for a long time. Be sure to post signs indicating everyone is warmly welcome at worship, education, and social events. Follow through on the community initiative..

Our call in baptism as members of the church is, in fact, a call to the vocation of evangelist-teacher or teacher-evangelist, wherever we are.

3. HOW DO WE MAKE THE GOSPEL COME ALIVE THROUGH EDUCATION AND EVANGELISM?

Carol R. Jacobson

Have you ever been on a mission or wanted to go on one? If so, perhaps you have imagined having experiences like the one Kent Knutson describes here:

> This summer I went on a trip. It was a wonderful trip and I haven't found my voice yet since I came back. At one place we went to a hospital. . . . I thought I would have a very nice time. I was aghast. As we went from room to room my heart sank deeper and deeper. I asked the doctor as we had finished the tour, "What is the greatest need you have?" and he said, "Water." Can you imagine a hospital without enough water? He showed me the well where the water had sunk almost out of sight. I did not say, "Let us pray." I did not say, "God will take care of you." God has given us some responsibilities. I went out and asked, "Where can we find a well digger?" I learned that there was one not far away and I told our business manager, "Bring him here." That is one way to make the gospel live. That is evangelism—to make the gospel alive.[1]

If we can imagine ourselves having this experience, I suspect we all hope that we would have done something similar—that we, too, would have done our best to find and pay a well digger for the hospital. But perhaps we are also a little afraid that we would not have, or *could not* have, done something like what Knutson was able to do. Wherever you may find yourself in this story, it is a powerful account of one Christian community's practice of evangelism, which, Knutson said, is about making the gospel come alive in our world today.

Evangelism is an intimidating word to many Christians. Like visiting the dentist, we know that evangelism is something we *should* do, but are often fearful about doing. We wonder, "Will I have to talk to strangers or do something that makes me uncomfortable?" "Will I know what to say?" "Will people even listen?" We protest that we are neither theologians nor pastors, and so we prefer to leave evangelism to the professionals. A brief look at any Lutheran baptismal rite reminds us, however, that evangelism is the vocation given to each of us at our baptism. We read, "We welcome you into the body of Christ and the mission we share. Join us as we give praise to God and bear God's creative and redeeming word to all the world."[2] Proclaiming the gospel to all the world—making it alive in our time and place—is each Christian's calling by virtue of his or her baptism.

> Everyone who has been given that grace, is an evangelist; and that means that it is everybody's business in the church. It isn't the preacher's business only, it isn't only the business of a department at the national offices or a committee in the congregation, it isn't a campaign, it isn't an emphasis, it isn't a gimmick, it isn't a program. It is the living out of the faith, the expression of the grace given to us.[3]

We are all called and empowered by God to be evangelists, beginning on our baptism day. For the sake of our baptismal calling, then, we must learn how to be evangelists.

Evangelism has not always been done well. Even though we are called and empowered by God to be evangelists, we rightly wonder, "Will I come off as judgmental or rude?" "Will people argue or disagree with me?" "Will it look like I have some kind of larger 'agenda'?" We protest that Christians have not always been good witnesses for the gospel and wonder if we could really do any better. And yet *it is you and me*, just as we are today, that God has called and equipped for this task. Trusting in God to strengthen the vocation of evangelist in us, we will consider three questions that can help us deepen our understanding of how we can be partners with God in making the gospel alive in the world. What exactly is the gospel to which we bear witness? How do we come to know the gospel for ourselves? And, finally, how can we bear witness to the gospel in our world today?

The Gospel as Power and Promise

What exactly is the gospel to which we bear witness? Answering this question may prove more difficult than we might initially think. One of my colleagues, Ted Peters, assigns students to write their first paper in his theology class addressing just this question, "What is the gospel?" Students discover worlds of scriptural witness, theological writing, hymnody, and art that provide answers to this question. They also discover, however, just how difficult it can be to articulate for *themselves* what the gospel is. The Greek word for "gospel," *euangelion*, means "good news." But good news about what? In the baptismal rite quoted earlier, the gospel is equated with God's "creative and redeeming Word." But where is this Word spoken to us? In the Bible? In church? In Jesus' crucifixion and resurrection? In receiving the Lord's Supper? God's creative and redeeming Word is heard and seen and touched and even tasted in all these places and more. But what exactly is this good news, and how do we know when we are hearing it?

Perhaps it helps to clarify for ourselves what the gospel is *not*. First of all, it is not a thing. The gospel is not an object, like the Golden Gate Bridge, to which one can point and say, "There it is over there." Rather, the gospel is an event, something that happens. Thinking of the gospel in this way helps us to remember that the gospel is God doing something, actively speaking a Word to all of us and to the whole world. The gospel is God's living Word that, in its proclamation, communicates the grace of God to us. It does so in two ways. First, proclaiming the gospel *reveals* to us God's gracious dealings with humanity in Jesus Christ, much in the way that a painting is revealed once the cloth that was covering it has been removed. Moreover, the gospel also *creates and deepens* Christian faith in the lives of all who hear it. By the power of God's Spirit, this gospel reaches into hearts, minds, and lives to teach, to challenge, to effect change, and to enable growth. Whenever the gospel is proclaimed, both education and evangelism occur. As Luther explains,

> No one can correctly understand God or His Word unless he has received such understanding immediately from the Holy Spirit. But no one can receive it from the Holy Spirit without experiencing, proving, or feeling it. In such experience, the Holy Spirit instructs us as in His own school, outside of which nothing is learned but empty words and prattle.[4]

The gospel, then, is a dynamic, moving, living phenomenon that captures and changes, that encompasses hope, love, destiny, power, and freedom.

The gospel is God's revelatory and creative Word of grace to us for the sake of Christ Jesus. It is living and active in the world today. It is a divine Word that accomplishes forgiveness, establishes justice, and grounds hope for the world. It is a divine Word that promises reconciliation, new life, and salvation for all who believe. This creative and redeeming Word—Jesus crucified and risen—is present and active wherever and whenever the gospel is made alive today.

The gospel Word is the content of all Christian education and the impetus of all Christian evangelism. Christian education and evangelism both exist to make the gospel alive in the world.

Because the gospel is a living Word that both reveals and acts to create, some theologians use the framework of narrative to help us better understand just how the gospel can be made alive in the world today. The gospel functions like any effective narrative or story. But there are limits to the ability of a narrative to adequately convey the revelatory and active dimensions of the event character of the gospel in the present tense.[5] By speaking of the gospel as story, we run the risk of focusing our attention on events we perceive to be primarily in the past, thereby potentially overlooking the presence and effective power of the gospel in our own time and place.

> The Gospel, then, is not a story but a power (Paul wrote this before the Gospel had become the Gospels). It is God's Spirit in us now, in the age of the Church, calling us to himself. . . . For the focus is not on the story, not on the past, but on Paul's "power of God unto salvation, first for the Jew, then for the Greek," and right now for you and me.[6]

The gospel is nothing other than God's Spirit alive in us now, calling us to lives of faithfulness, hope, and love. It is, as Paul says, the power of God at work to both reveal and effect salvation—for you, for me, and for the cosmos.[7]

The gospel is an event, a power that is present and active in the world. And, as Luther would remind us, the gospel is also a profound promise. It is God's Word of promise that, because of Jesus Christ, reconciliation, new life, and salvation have been freely given by God to all. Likewise, evangelization and education are also an event—God active through and among people in the proclamation of and living out of the gospel. As Luther writes,

> For God does not deal, nor has he ever dealt, with man *[sic]* otherwise than through a word of promise, as I have said. We in turn cannot deal with God otherwise than through faith in the Word of his promise. He does not desire works, nor has he need of them; rather we deal with men and with ourselves on the basis of works. But God has need of this: that we consider him faithful to his promises [Heb. 10:23]. . . . It is in this way that he obtains his glory among us, since it is not of ourselves who run, but of him who shows mercy [Rom. 9:16], promises, and gives, that we have and hold all good things.[8]

What is this gospel promise? It is nothing other than God's own promise to "mend the entire universe,"[9] as pastor and theologian Dan Erlander puts it. Or, in the words of Paul, the gospel is God's promise both to "reconcile us to himself through Christ" and to entrust "the message of reconciliation to us."[10] The content of this promise is the reconciliation, new life, and salvation—that divine event for the mending of the universe—wrought in Jesus Christ. And now the message has been entrusted to us to be taught, caught, and shared. In order to bear witness to the power and the promise of the gospel, however, we must first come to know and trust its power and promise for ourselves and in our own lives.

Knowing the Power and the Promise of the Gospel for Ourselves

When did we first hear about Jesus? Was it in church? Was it at home? However we first heard about Jesus, at that very moment, we began to know the gospel for ourselves. But what does it really mean to know the gospel for oneself? How can we be sure that the power and promise of the gospel is truly power and promise for us?

We must first recognize that knowing the gospel in this way will be different than simply knowing *about* the gospel. To truly know the power and promise of the gospel *for oneself* suggests a way of knowing that is fundamentally relational. This way of knowing both presupposes the involvement of our whole selves and trusts in God's promise to be present to us and in us through the Spirit. God and faith belong together in this way of knowing. As the biblical writers and Jesus himself remind us, to know in this way means to "love the Lord your God with all your heart, and with all your soul, and with all your mind, and with all your strength."[11] Heart, soul, mind, and strength are all involved in knowing the power and the promise of the gospel for ourselves. Christian education recognizes and celebrates the involvement of the entire self (and, indeed, the whole faith community) in the practices of learning to know the gospel for ourselves. Christian educational practices are always operating, therefore, on cognitive, affective, and active levels. In this way, the gospel is made alive in minds, hearts, and communities.

At the center of our attention in this way of knowing "is a subject (that is, the gospel) that continually calls us deeper into its secret, a subject that refuses to be reduced to our conclusions about it."[12] Knowing the gospel for ourselves, then, is much like knowing another person. To know in this way . . . "is to allow one's self to be known as well, to be vulnerable to the challenges and changes any true relationship brings. To know in truth is to enter into the life of that which we know and to allow it to enter into ours."[13] This describes what is at the heart of both good educational practices and effective evangelizing efforts. To know in this way is to trust. Knowing the gospel's power and promise for ourselves means allowing ourselves to be known by this gospel, to be open to change on account of it, and to hold nothing of ourselves back from it. God desires nothing more than to know and to be known by us in this intimate, incarnate, and trusting way. The birth, death, and resurrection of Jesus reveal this to us, as Robert Taft explains:

> Christmas is not just about the coming of Christ to Bethlehem, but about the coming of Christ to me, and about my going out to others. And Easter is not about the empty tomb in Jerusalem some 2,000 years ago, but about the reawakening here and now of my baptismal death and resurrection in Christ."[14]

Knowing the gospel for ourselves means Christmas and Easter are not just about past events and promises, but are the ways in which God comes to and for us today and continues to come into every time and into all of history.

We may feel, however, that there is much about our lives that gets in the way of remaining connected with God and with the power of the gospel promise in this intimate way. Like Saint Paul, we must admit that, while our spirits are willing, our flesh often struggles to find time and space for knowing God in the midst of a busy week. We manage to carve out time for worship on Sunday, perhaps, but wish that our prayer life could be better and that we connected faith more fully with our daily lives. We can well understand the frustration of a young mother, who said to author Kathleen Norris one Sunday morning,

> "I've just begun finding my way back to all this," she said, "and I think you can help me." . . . She was longing for a relationship with God but didn't know how to go about it. How to pray, for example. . . . She told me that she didn't know how to get started, but her little girl seemed to talk to God all the time. "There you have it," I said, "just imitate her." And she laughed. I was being partly seriously, I told her, because adult self-consciousness makes

us more anxious than we need to be about "seeking God." . . . Just relax, I told her, don't worry, and if you begin to read the Bible you'll find that if you think you want to find God, God wants to find you even more.[15]

A good place to begin to know God's gospel in the midst of our day-to-day lives is to first relax and try not to worry that we are not doing enough, or not doing it right. It is not up to us to create the gospel's presence in our lives—this God has promised to do and will do.

Next, we must begin to recognize the active presence of the gospel in our lives. Since we can hear God's gospel Word spoken in many places—in church, in Bible study, in prayer—there are many opportunities for us to practice recognizing the gospel's activity in everyday life. Where is God active in our lives today? There, the gospel is being made alive.

Studying the biblical witness to the power and promise of the gospel is also vital to learning to recognize its presence in everyday life. In the Scriptures, God's Word is spoken to us afresh, and we encounter there numerous accounts of men and women, boys and girls, who have heard that same Word in the day-to-day events of their lives. Studying the biblical witness can take many forms—Bible study, active church participation, daily devotional texts, reading before bed, small group conversation. In whatever form, engagement with the Scriptures enhances our recognition of the gospel as it is made alive in our world today.

Similarly, the practice of prayer strengthens our awareness of the power and presence of the gospel in our daily lives. Like studying the Scriptures, prayer can be practiced in a myriad of ways and at any time. It is both an individual practice and a corporate one. Some prayers have words; others are silent. However one prays, God's availability to us in prayer is a divine promise in which we can trust. Cultivating practices of prayer in daily life opens us up to the power and promise of the gospel alive in today's world. Prayer schools our awareness (education) and makes the gospel alive (evangelism) whenever it occurs.

Receiving the Lord's Supper also teaches us to recognize and to give thanks for the gospel made alive among us and for us. It is at the Lord's table that we learn how deeply God in Jesus Christ loves us and all people. Each time we receive the Lord's Supper, we taste and see the power and the promise of the gospel's Word of forgiveness, reconciliation, and peace. We hear the gospel's call to be witnesses to it with the whole of our lives—we are evangelists. And we learn, once again, that the fruit of the sacrament is love of God and neighbor. Luther's Post Communion Prayer expresses it this way:

We give you thanks, almighty God, that you have refreshed us through the healing power of this gift of life; and we pray that in your mercy you would strengthen us, through this gift, in faith toward you and in fervent love toward one another; for the sake of Jesus Christ our Lord. Amen.[16]

To receive the Lord's Supper is to be called, once again, to be a learner, a teacher, and an evangelist, helping to make the gospel alive in the world by loving one's neighbor.

Bearing Witness to the Power and the Promise of the Gospel with Our Lives

> My life flows on in endless song; above earth's lamentation,
> I catch the sweet, though far-off hymn that hails a new creation.
> Through all the tumult and the strife, I hear that music ringing.
> It finds an echo in my soul. How can I keep from singing?[17]

Learning to recognize the gospel as alive and active in one's whole life is not a matter of private piety and practice alone. Of necessity, it involves both public witness and private practices of discipleship. Like the hymn writer cited above, we who have come to know the gospel's promise and power "find an echo" in our souls—one that compels us to share that living and life-giving Word with those in the world around us. We recognize that we cannot "keep from singing" about all that God in Christ has done for us. Central to the biblical witness and to Lutheran theological understandings is this essential connection between knowing and loving God and knowing and loving our neighbors.

In his Post Communion prayer, Luther directly addresses the essential connection that exists between God's gift of faith to us, on the one hand, and our responsibility for loving our neighbors on the other. These two are intimately and inextricably related. In his treatise, "On the Freedom of a Christian," Luther employs the imagery of flowing water and of clothing oneself in order to further describe this mutually correlative relationship between love of God and love of neighbor. He writes,

> [T]he good things we have from God should flow from one to the other and be common to all, so that everyone should "put on" his neighbor and so conduct himself toward him as if he himself were in the other's place. From Christ the good things have flowed and are flowing into us. He has so "put on" us and acted for us as if he had been what we are. From us they flow on to those who have need of them so that I should lay before God my faith and my righteousness that they may cover and intercede for the sins of my neighbor which I take upon myself and so labor and serve in them as if they were my very own. That is what Christ did for us. This is true love and the genuine role of a Christian life. . . . We conclude, therefore, that a Christian lives not in himself, but in Christ and in his neighbor. Otherwise he is not a Christian. He lives in Christ through faith, in his neighbor through love.[18]

All those who have come to know the gospel's power and promise, Luther says, no longer live turned in upon themselves, but rather they live "outside of themselves" in Christ and in their neighbors. The good things we have from God—grace, faith, forgiveness, salvation—flow from Christ to us, Luther explains. At the same time, they flow out from us "to those who have need of them"—that is, to our world filled with more neighbors than we can count.

Luther speaks of the way in which Christ loved and served humanity by "putting us on" as one would put on a piece of clothing. God in Christ became human for the sake of the salvation of the world, remaining faithful to the fulfilling of the gospel's own promise. In the same way, Luther says, we are called to "put on" our neighbors and work diligently to support their flourishing in faith and life. This calling to live outside of ourselves in God and neighbor is a good way of understanding what it means to be an evangelist. Living this way *is* evangelism, and it is *education* for the neighbor in the very broadest sense of that term.

Certainly living outside oneself does not mean that we are meant to dissociate from ourselves or neglect ourselves somehow. Luther is speaking about something other than that. Living outside of ourselves is God's gift to us, a gift that God alone makes possible. It is the gift of and the calling to a lifetime of learning and evangelism. This way of living is how God speaks gospel power and promise in every age—by calling and equipping men, women, boys, and girls as partners in the ongoing divine work of reconciliation. This partnership with God in Christ is what Luther meant by Christians living outside of themselves and in Christ. The gift of this partnership flows from Christ to us, and it flows through us to help us serve our neighbors.

Evangelism is nothing other than making the gospel alive in the world today by living outside of ourselves in Christ and neighbor. The gospel is a living power and faithful promise that both reveals God's salvation for all in Christ and acts in history and human lives to accomplish it. In order to bear witness to this gospel, we must first discover and come to depend upon the power and the promise of the gospel for our own lives and in our daily living. For this reason, lifelong Christian education of mind, body, soul, and strength are essential to the vocation of the evangelist. What we learn through such education is not a program or a to-do list, but rather a pattern for Christian living to which we have been called and for which we have been equipped by God's grace. God calls us to live outside of our self-preoccupation and to participate in genuine Christian living. When Christians live in this way, the gospel is made alive. We are evangelists. Called at our baptism, we are made partners with God that we might continue to grow in that faith through lifelong Christian education and to bear witness to the gospel's power and promise to heal brokenness of every kind, including our own. Living in faith toward God and in fervent love toward one another gives expression in daily life to the grace that has been given to us by God in Christ though the power of the Holy Spirit.

Questions for Reflection and Conversation

1. Who first told you the story of Jesus? How old were you? What can you remember about your first conversations about Jesus?

2. Is there someone you know who is longing to hear about the love and forgiveness God offers in Jesus Christ? Consider including this person in your prayers. What could you do to reach out to this person?

Parish Strategies

1. As a congregation, invite each group in your congregation to address the following: "What do you still need in order to live more fully into your vocation as a lifelong learner and evangelist?" After identifying these needs, make a list of concrete strategies to address these challenges.

2. Does your congregation have a mission statement? A vision statement? If not, begin a conversation about developing such statements. If so, do they adequately reflect your congregation's present understanding of itself as an educating and evangelizing church? How might the statements be changed to emphasize more fully the church's call to grow in and bear witness to the gospel?

> *Proclaiming the gospel to all the world—making it alive in our time and place—is each Christian's calling by virtue of his or her baptism.*

4. HOW DO WE MOVE FROM APATHY TO TRANSFORMATION?

Donald R. Just

Growing up in the church, I have heard about "evangelism" since early childhood. The spreading and sharing of the good news of salvation is understood to be an expectation of the congregation. The words of the great commission, "Go therefore and make disciples of all nations, baptizing them in the name of the Father and the Son and the Holy Spirit, and teaching them to obey everything that I have commanded you" (Mt 28:19-20) were nearly as well known to most congregants as the words from John 3:16: "For God so loved the world that he gave his only Son, so that everyone who believes in him may have eternal life." However, except for contributions to domestic and foreign mission programs, I don't ever recall the congregation acting on the mandate of the great commission with much enthusiasm. In retrospect, I have often wondered if the expectation of evangelism didn't engender more guilt than anything else.

Perhaps it was a case of effective preaching not being properly complemented by an equally effective parish education program. It seems that we heard the words of the great commission primarily as divine mandate and command. Without the benefit of an education program about the intent and promise of the great commission, it became a burden laid upon us by a demanding God.

Later, in my work as a parish pastor and as a chaplain in military and in church-college settings, I would regularly raise the matter of our response to the mandate of the great commission with seemingly little response. There was general agreement that the work of evangelism was an expectation of the congregation and believers, but this fostered little response other than relatively minor financial contributions made to global missions or new local mission congregations through offerings and benevolences. There were any number of training sessions and workshops on how we might better invite our friends and neighbors to worship with us or instruction sessions on how to knock on neighborhood doors with brochures in-hand and an invitation to check us out. Here, I wonder if our educational efforts were not too focused on technique without the benefit of a sound theological rationale about the work of outreach.

Somewhere through these experiences, I came to the conclusion that evangelism was rarely anyone's gift. It seemed that many, if not most, of the people that participated in neighborhood outreach efforts with me did not have the gift for evangelism, or it was simply too far outside of their comfort zone. It was not for lack of trying. Indeed, most of the parishioners were willing workers in the congregation. They willingly and gladly served on committees, worked in the kitchen and on the grounds, ushered, quilted, folded bulletins, served as greeters, assisted with worship, taught Sunday school and so on. But doing evangelism—that was not their thing.

Still, I believe that, for most people nurtured in the Christian faith, sharing and proclaiming the faith is understood as a given. Christians have been invited, urged, and encouraged in many ways and many times to share the good news of God's gracious love in Jesus Christ. People have a general understanding that education should lead to evangelism. They have been asked repeatedly to invite their neighbor to worship and to announce worship events and other activities of the congregation. They have been asked to support prayerfully and financially the work of the church, which has included evangelism programs.

Evangelism as a Program of the Congregation

Part of the problem with evangelism in many congregations is that it is seen as one of many programmatic expectations. To be sure, all are important to the life of the congregation. But is evangelism just another congregational program? When all programs and expectations in the congregation are seen as important, as they should be, is it the case that maintenance of facilities, staff salaries, worship, and social ministry take top priority, or at least the most attention, while education and evangelism are left behind because people can respond effectively and do well with only so many programs or expectations?

There seems to be a pretty serious disconnect between the expectation that Christians are to proclaim and share the Gospel and their response to that expectation. Given the apparent apathy toward outreach, perhaps it is time to ask whether evangelism is really all that important after all. I recall watching a television news interview program on television years ago that involved some of the leading news reporters of the Vietnam War era. Today, such a discussion could very well be about Iraq. One veteran reporter, in particular, spoke of attending numerous press conferences during that time in which all the questions posed to presidents, secretaries of defense, field commanders, and other high-ranking officials repeatedly dealt with war strategy and tactics—matters such as weaponry, enemy movements, troop numbers, and so on. The reporter's regret was that neither he nor anyone else ever asked the most important question: "Why are we in Vietnam in the first place?" There was agreement among the television program guests that the press had failed in this regard. It seems that the Church, too, has been talking about evangelism programs and outreach methodology without asking more important questions: "Why be concerned about evangelism at all? Is all the energy, anxiety, and guilt even necessary?"

Still, the question seems like an odd one. For most Christians, the answer is obvious. We have the great commission as a biblical imperative. We have Jesus' words to his followers that, "you shall be witnesses in Jerusalem, in all Judea and Samaria, and all the ends of the earth" (Acts 1:8). We have the promise that we shall receive power from the Holy Spirit to do it. Additionally, we have the authority of tradition that the good news is to be proclaimed. Otherwise:

> [H]ow are they to call on one in whom they have not believed? And how are they to believe in one of whom they have never heard? And how are they to hear without someone to proclaim him? And how are they to proclaim him unless they are sent? As it is written, "How beautiful are the feet of those who bring the good news!" (Rom. 10:14-15)

Furthermore, we have the examples of Paul and other apostles and missionaries being sent to the corners of the world to make known the good news to all people regardless of nationality or station.

So why is evangelism not happening? At least two, somewhat related factors need to be taken into account. First, in our postmodern world, there are unique obstacles to gospel proclamation that we need to overcome (an issue more fully explored in other chapters in this book). And secondly, it is an audacious message which we proclaim.

We live in a society where all truth is generally believed to be subjective and relative. The belief that any objective truth can be known has been jettisoned. Instead, we have settled for a subjective view of truth, which makes it merely personal and relative. One may argue that something may be "truth for me" or "truth for you," but not "truth for everyone."[1] Additionally there is the ongoing temptation to determine truth by "popular vote," that is, truth is determined by the number of people that believe it.

So if we believe that the gospel really is the good news that has a transformative power to change lives for the better, we are making a claim which, for many, has no objective or universal basis. We are left to celebrate "truth" as a personal gift, and leave it at that. In a culture where subjectivity and relativism reign, the claim that the good news is good for everyone else is rejected.

The writer of the Letter to the Corinthians acknowledged and understood that there is an "inherent foolishness" and audacious quality to a proclamation that runs so counter to the conventional wisdom of humanity. Paul wrote of the paradoxical element in God's revelation in his first letter to the Corinthians:

> The message of the cross is foolishness to those who are perishing, but to us who are being saved it is the power of God. . . . For God's foolishness is wiser than human wisdom, and God's weakness is stronger than human strength. (1:18 & 25.)

Such is the nature of evangelizing—to proclaim the foolishness of the cross as a universal truth to a subjective world. Given the daunting nature of that task, perhaps we have been too hard on ourselves for being less than successful.

Evangelism—Not Just Another Program

There are voices that claim that a major failure in our understanding of evangelism is that we too often see it as just another program of the church. They would argue that evangelism is not a program, but a way of being. Evangelism programs aren't enough. In fact, theologian Craig Nessan argues that programs are the death of evangelism. Instead, he calls for an engagement in an evangelizing culture "so rooted in our identity as a church that speaking the name of Jesus Christ and telling the story of what God has done for us will become as natural as talking about our families."[2]

Evangelism—what is it? Carol Jacobson, in chapter three of this volume, has already given us a working definition of gospel or evangelism. Still, here is another brief look at *euangelion*. It is an ancient Christian term derived from New Testament Greek word meaning "the gospel" as God's good news for the promise of salvation to all who have faith in Christ. It means, quite literally *ev* to *angel*—announcing the good news of salvation through faith in Jesus Christ and telling others how lives have been transformed through this faith.

Once the gospel is understood as good news to be announced to the world, the great commission is seen as more than a divine mandate. We are not so much ordered to be witnesses as we find "the love of Christ urges us on, because we are convinced that one has died for all; therefore all have died. And he died for all, so that those who live might live no longer for themselves, but for him who died and was raised for them" (2 Cor. 5: 14-15). If we need a good reason for doing evangelism, the key to that reason is "to understand the connection between the gift of salvation through Christ and the call to follow Christ. There is nothing we have to do—or even can do—to deserve the call to follow Christ. It is a gift. But let us also be clear: the gift we are given in Christ is a call."[3]

The apostle Paul wrote that, by virtue of our relationship with Jesus Christ, we are saved and set free from sin and death, and that nothing in creation will ever be able to take that away from us—nothing will ever be able to separate us from the love of God in Jesus Christ our Lord (Rom. 8). Having been set free, we belong to Christ (I Cor. 3:21) in order that we may bear fruit for God (Rom. 7:4). Such is the free gift of salvation.

Today, Christians are challenged to make sense of this confession and experience of Jesus as Lord and Savior in the context of missionary encounters with world religions and modern ideologies. We are expected to be ready to give the reason for the hope that is in us, to witness credibly to our belief that Jesus means God's own salvation, not only for ourselves, but for the whole world and all those who do not yet believe in his name. We go out "believing that the Spirit of God will open our lips to ways of proclaiming the gospel and new ways of naming Jesus."[4]

For theologian Carl Braaten, the church is missionary by nature. Just as God is a missionary God, so the church is to be a missionary church. This is the fundamental meaning behind the four attributes of the church confessed in the Apostles' Creed: one, holy, catholic, and apostolic. . . . The church's very posture of "sentness" creates a missionary dynamic in the world. God sent the Son into the world with a mission; the Spirit is sent by the Father and the Son with a mission; and now the church, baptized in the name of this Triune God, is being sent on a mission in the world under the direction of the Holy Spirit. Early twentiety-century theologian Emil Brunner wrote, "The Church exists by mission, just as a fire exists by burning."[5] It is in the church's DNA to be a witnessing church.

The Word of God, which was given in Jesus Christ, is a unique, historical fact, and everything Christian is dependent on it. Hence, everyone who receives this Word, and salvation through it, receives the duty of passing it on; just as a man who might have discovered a remedy that saved him from cancer would be duty-bound to make the remedy accessible to all.[6]

Education for Evangelism as Transformation

So we know in our heads that we have this gospel imperative to proclaim the good news to all of our neighbors, near and far. That is not new information to those in the church. So what will move us out of our comfort zones and into public discourse about the person and work of Jesus Christ? It seems that something of a transformative nature needs to happen to move us in that direction.

Over the years, I have served as a spiritual director for numerous spiritual renewal weekends. With adults, it was Via de Cristo programs in North Carolina and Texas. With high-school youth, it was Happening, and with college students it was Pathways. Via de Cristo, Happening, and Pathways are all modeled, in some way, after Cursillo, a spiritual renewal program developed by Roman Catholics in Spain. *Cursillo* means "short course," thus the renewal experience is designed to review the essentials of the catechism. This review of the faith takes place in the context of meaningful worship, silence, joyful music, fellowship, and dynamic instruction.

Something transformative happened on each of those weekends so that, for days following the experience, participants were just bursting to share with their friends a word about their renewed relationship with Jesus Christ. It was as though each of them had experienced the "were not our hearts burning within us" phenomenon of the disciples on the road to Emmaus described by Luke in chapter 24 of his Gospel. In these retreat settings, the participants, again, experienced the person of Jesus Christ in a unique and meaningful way, and out of appreciation and gratitude for the gift of grace they felt moved to share the good news of salvation with others.

Church bodies with their network of outdoor ministry facilities have been offering spiritual renewal experiences for decades. Many clergy, as well as other professional leaders in church bodies, credit a camping experience as the event that changed their lives by transforming their relationships with God. As a result, many would become proclaimers of the gospel. Still others would become better equipped to take up vocations of service in their communities. This is, indeed, a form of education that results in providing able communicators of the good news of the gospel.

When a Story Needs to Be Told

Perhaps it is the nature of humans to want to share good news with others. A friend tells of his experience of becoming a father for the first time. He recalls that, after spending some time in a hospital room with his wife and newborn son, he left the room to find a telephone to tell their families the good news. He called his parents, but got no answer. He called in-laws, but no one answered the telephone. He called his sister, but she was not home either. On the way back home, he stopped for some grocery items. It was there he found a stranger to whom he could say, "I'm a father!" The woman was gracious, and offered her congratulations. He had been bursting to tell someone the good news. Then, there is the story of the recluse woman who lived alone. She inherited a huge sum of money. Since she had no friends, she picked up the phone book and called strangers to tell them her good news. She, too, had to tell someone.

The participants in a spiritual-renewal weekend, the new father, and the reclusive woman all had good news to share. Something prompted them to do more than keep it to themselves. All needed to share that news with someone. The motivation seemed to be the joy and gratitude they experienced over their good fortune. With the good news of the gospel, it is not just our need to tell the story of Christ's love, but the belief that the good news will bring joy and gratitude into the lives of others as well.

Another colleague tells of a time when he was traveling and happened to be wearing his clerical collar. A fellow traveler, upon seeing the collar, proceeded to tell him that he "didn't have much use for religion." But for some unknown reason, the traveler was also prompted to ask my friend why he thought Christianity merited any serious attention. My colleague, seeing an opportunity to give witness, responded by telling his fellow traveler that, in his experience, no other story but the Christian story so completely reflected who he was. He continued, "Bible stories don't whitewash who we as humans are." David, Cain, Abraham, Joseph, Jezebel, Isaac, and Jacob were all scoundrels in one form or another. These biblical stories are about people with faults. When looking at these stories, we really see ourselves.

Even more important, we see a God who is absolutely free to do whatever the divine heart desires. Yet, this is a God who remains absolutely faithful. The story of the covenant is about the faithfulness of God, and so it is a story of hope. My colleague further noted that in his life journey, he had read stories that described him very well, but gave him no hope. Further, he had read stories that offered hope but did not describe him. Scripture contains stories that do both: they describe us as we are, warts and all, and they give us hope for the journey. So Christianity is not so much about doing this or that—but about our freedom to grapple with and articulate our own faith in the world. This is the audacity of education as evangelism.

So, despite the belief of many that they do not have much use for religion, and probably not with one identified by the symbol of a cross, there is an overriding belief shared with C. S. Lewis that, "there is a void in each of us that only Christ can fill," and that there is deep, deep longing within humanity to which only the gospel speaks and to which only the gospel can give hope. As bearers of good news, we have a response to that longing that gives hope to the world.

Educators who are people of the promise have a unique opportunity to help brothers and sisters appreciate the importance of evangelism and witness in the life-of-faith communities. We are not concerned only with the means by which the message is shared, but with the "why" of sharing it. We need, foremost, to answer the question, Why is evangelism important at all? What compels us to tell the story of faith to others? Then, convinced that the promise of salvation is real, we go forth with the further assurance that, "My word that goes out from my mouth; it shall not return empty, but shall accomplish that which I purpose, and succeed in the thing for which I sent it" (Isa. 55:11). Finally, Christian educators become key participants in a movement across the church in which evangelism will no longer be one program or ministry functioning alongside others, but integral to them all. Central to the educational task is fostering evangelizing cultures in which our way of speaking and acting will naturally include "speaking the name of Jesus Christ and telling the story of what God has done for us."[7]

Questions for Reflection and Conversation

1. What is your understanding of the "gospel imperative" to be a witness to the work of Jesus Christ in your life and the life of your communities?

2. Think of some settings in which you have shared parts of your life story with friends or acquaintances. What made it possible for you to do that?

3. While sharing a part of your life story with friends or acquaintances, how were you able to speak of God's activity or the activity of your faith community in your life?

Parish Strategies

1. Imagine a congregational culture in which evangelism is not seen as the activity or program of just one committee or the pastoral staff. What might that look like? How might education and evangelism be linked and integrated throughout the entire congregational culture? Make some concrete plans to do so.

2. Sit down with a group of people and share honestly some negative images of evangelism that various members of the group have, for example, fundamentalist groups giving a hard sell at the door. What might you learn from these experiences, either positively or negatively? Engage in an educational experience of role play to practice putting into words some life-giving ways of actually talking with people about your faith in Christ.

Without the benefit of an education program about the intent and promise of the great commission, it became a burden laid upon us by a demanding God.

PART TWO

EXPLORING THE POSSIBILITIES

5. CONGREGATIONS THAT TAKE BOTH EDUCATION AND EVANGELISM SERIOUSLY

_____

Mary E. Hughes

Six-year-old Spencer came to church last Sunday. In Sunday school, he heard the story of Jesus who died on a cross, then rose again to give life after death. He took home two tiny crosses with the suggestion to share one of the crosses and tell the Jesus story to someone else. So he did. He went across the street to visit Mrs. Golden saying, "I have a story to tell you." He told her about how Jesus had died on a cross, and then rose again so that she could have life. And Spencer gave her the tiny cross as a reminder.

Later in the week, Mrs. Golden was in the checkout lane at Wal-Mart. When she opened her purse, the cashier asked about the tiny cross Mrs. Golden was carrying with her change. So Mrs. Golden told the cashier about Spencer and the story Spencer had told her. Then she gave the cross to the cashier. For the rest of the week, the cashier wore the cross on a name tag. I wonder who has asked her about that cross, and I wonder if she told about Spencer, Mrs. Golden, and the story they told.

The shocking thing about this story is that it is surprising. In fact, it represents just what we hope happens in the lives of Christians. We hear the gospel, and we share the gospel. We enter the church building to worship and learn. We leave the church building to live and share a life lived in Jesus. It is our hope that, when others see a life lived faithfully and hear the story of Jesus, they, too, will want to hear more and learn more and become part of the community of faith. The connection between education and evangelism may be the most natural relationship in ministry. Education and evangelism make wonderful partners.

The Christian Education-Evangelism Connection

What happens when a congregation takes seriously the call to educate and the call to evangelize? Can congregations do both well? Can one happen without the other?

The stories on the following pages illustrate ministries that seriously attempt to integrate Christian education and evangelism. Each story is different. There are many ways to live out this vital relationship. All reveal various shapes to the education-evangelism connection. The following principles undergird the stories:

1. Christian education helps people live faithful lives every day, and the everyday lives of Christians are witness to the gospel of Jesus Christ. A life lived in faith is one's strongest witness to that faith. In a nutshell, the Christian life is an evangelizing life. Christian education helps the Christian at each age explore just what it means to live as a Christian in everyday life.

2. When those around us ask about our faith or our faithful lives, we have a story to tell. Christian education helps the Christian know the story and know how to share the story.

3. When persons are hungry for the gospel and hungry for a relationship with God, Christian education is one natural place to turn to hear, to explore, to question, and to investigate. Christian education is an essential part of the formation of Christians, especially new and renewing Christians.

4. As persons engage the gospel, they are moved both toward deeper study and toward sharing their faith. In Christian education, the faithful dig deeper, seeking meaning, seeking to know what it means to live faithfully in a complex work. As one digs deeply into the gospel, he or she finds the words and discovers the drive to share the faith.

Gracious Saviour Lutheran Church, Detroit

Gracious Saviour Lutheran Church in Detroit, Michigan, organized in 1961, dwindled in numbers during the dramatic population shifts of the 1960s and 1970s. By 1990, worship attendance averaged about twenty-five people/congregants. Committees were not meeting. There had been no quorum for church council in six months.

Gracious Saviour was a neighborhood church. In the surrounding neighborhood, there were large, metropolitan churches, but this smaller congregation became the gathering-place church. Alcoholics Anonymous, Block Clubs, community-organizing groups, and other community groups met there regularly. Not truly an inner-city church, Gracious Saviour was in northwest Detroit in a middle class neighborhood of brick homes built in the mid-twentieth century. The white population had left quickly and almost completely, so that by 1970, the community was mostly African American. The congregation was established in 1961 as the merger of two churches. The new sanctuary and fellowship hall were wonderful. However, the education building, which was the old sanctuary, had a bad roof and needed expensive repair.

When Pastor Carla Nelson became pastor in December 1990, she found three noticeable strengths on which to build: (1) children's education, (2) youth ministry, and (3) music.

There were only four children who regularly came to Sunday school, but six teachers were already there, waiting for children to come. Even as the church struggled, lay leaders did not give up the familiar structure of Sunday school, and it was to that Sunday school that the community would be invited.

Some people say that Lutherans do not evangelize through the Sunday school, but that was not true at Gracious Saviour. This congregation, through its new pastor and members, went out looking for children for a Sunday school already in place with waiting, willing teachers. When children came to the church, they brought with them family, extended family, and friends. The children brought new members to the church.

Youth knew this church to be a safe place that was open a lot, and the children of the neighborhood recognized the car of Pastor Carla, as she was addressed around the church and community. The church paved the gravel parking lot to make walking easier and to create an outdoor gym with a basketball court.

Twenty-five years earlier, Gracious Saviour's pastor had walked the neighborhood and built up a ministry among youth and their families. Now these youth were adult members of the congregation, and they walked the neighborhood inviting the community to come to Gracious Saviour.

While the building was not suitable for activities, the members had a heart for children and youth. When the church had to turn away kids at Vacation Bible School because of a lack of space, the members said, "This is ridiculous. We can't do that." This was the beginning of the campaign to renovate the education building.

Adults in the neighborhood were interested in the children and youth. If an adult was sitting on the porch, a young person did not walk by without the adult speaking. Children knew this expectation, so they stopped for conversation. They knew the adult would ask about school and the latest report card. Children used the relational address of Miss, Mr., Uncle, Aunt, Brother, and Sister with the adults around them. It was a sign of respect and a sign of relationship.

The neighborhood interest in children became the church's interest in these children. Several of the homes of Gracious Saviour's members had doors open to the youth of the neighborhood. On Sunday morning, you would see five, seven, eight children jump out of a neighbor's car and run up the church steps. At church, children would be greeted with respect and interest, and there, too, they would be asked about their report cards. These children knew they belonged to the community and that they belonged in worship. Intentionally, no separate nursery was provided, although parents could spend a few minutes with children in the narthex if necessary. In a congregation of one hundred worshippers, thirty-five children would run up front for the children's sermon.

Adults in the church and in the neighborhood would watch their children with great joy. It is an uplifting feeling to watch young people run to the church door. The parents followed their children to this church, where the children and youth learned and knew love and respect.

Re-development at Gracious Saviour did not take place quickly, but one could sense a renewing spirit. In about seven years, the growth was recognizable. According to Pastor Carla, "We grew because we did the best we could in education, youth work and music. We engaged in this ministry not for growth in and of itself but for faithfulness and people came."

What did faithfulness mean at Gracious Saviour in that situation with those strengths? It meant relational ministry with children and youth, often enhanced with the informal creation of small groups. It meant repeated and varied invitations to the community to join their children at this place. It meant challenging and interesting opportunities for Bible study. In worship, faithfulness meant praising God, singing the songs of the context and culture, telling Bible stories, and naming the name of Jesus. Pastor Carla's mantra was, "Bring Jesus to people and bring people to Jesus."

Pastor Carla was challenged to develop and use her gift for teaching. On Sunday mornings, she taught new-member classes; on weekdays she taught Bible studies. She worked hard to become an excellent Bible teacher, and adults trusted she could teach them things. In her fifteen years of ministry she taught forty-five books of the Bible. Bible studies were held four times a week, and today there are many adults who could "hold their own" in any seminary Bible class. The weekday classes naturally created small groups in which members developed the relational ministry dear to this church. When a study group became larger than twelve, a new group was started.

Music remained an important component of dynamic worship at Gracious Saviour. A similar relational approach was used in this music ministry. To include more people in music ministry, the current choir continued, but new choirs were added . . . eventually totaling five.

The adults at Gracious Saviour cared about their adolescents. The relationships forged between youth and adults kept the teens coming to church. Their relationships would remain the foundation of youth ministry.

What Is Going on Here?

Education and evangelism at Gracious Saviour match this church's history, context, and gifts. One could focus on the negatives: small numbers, a building needing repair, bigger churches just around the corner, population shifts along racial lines, and low energy. Or one could see the positives: members who are neighborhood "hubs;" a Sunday school structure waiting for participants; identity as a small, neighborhood gathering place; a community and members who share a genuine interest in their children and youth.

Add to that a pastoral leader willing to commit years of energetic ministry to this church and community. Pastor Carla reports, "It took so long, I think, because Gracious Saviour had to teach me how to pastor in a culture and tradition different from my own. I had wonderful mentors and teachers, members of Gracious Saviour, colleagues, and pastors who were patient and forgiving of my mistakes."

One cannot separate education and evangelism at Gracious Saviour. There is the continuous outreach of inviting and welcoming children, who then bring their families and friends. Thoughtful, nurturing education awaits children and adults who come.

Without a vital ministry, why invite others? Without invitations, who will come? When new persons come, what will they find? When they find faithfulness and opportunities for growth, they return. When they return, the whole faith community is enriched.

Christ Lutheran Church, Bexley, Ohio

There's a grand experiment working at Christ Church. This large, stable congregation within an affluent inner suburbof Columbus, OH, has a history of broad and varied ministries. In recent years, however, church leaders sensed they were on a "wilderness journey," with low energy and little sense of direction. Last spring, the council appointed a vision team, and a new vision statement was adopted: "Challenging Everyone to Experience an Adventurous Life with Christ Now."

A new pastor was installed in August. Pastor Tim quickly picked up on the vision statement, helping the congregation strategize how to live that vision. Heidi, the Director of Christian Education for several years, had a good grasp of the current ministry, available resources, and congregational dynamics. Soon, one could hear energizing conversations among staff, within committees, in church council, and in informal hallway chats.

The ministries at Christ could be described as "siloed," that is, each committee did its own thing with little interaction or overlap between events or activities. As committees talked about the vision statement, the Adult Education Committee began to talk to the Spiritual Growth Group. Soon Social Action was joining with Evangelism in organizing activities. As committees talked with one another, they all participated in implementing the vision statement. A discipleship theme has emerged for the coming year: "Being disciples, making disciples . . . the adventure begins."

Two questions lay a foundation for this discipleship theme: Who are we as people of God? Who are we as a church? To help members answer those questions, three opportunities for education and growth are planned. They form the strategy for implementing the vision statement in the near future.

1. Bible 101. This is a long-term, large-group adult Bible study, with a trained leader providing foundational knowledge of the Bible for new Christians and a refresher course for others. Decades ago, the congregation had a good experience with a long-term, intensive Bible study, so when Pastor Tim suggested offering another long-term Bible study, he could build on good memories. Because he was already trained as a leader of that study, he was ready to begin a nine-month study quickly, within two months.

The decision to offer Bible 101 recognizes every Christian's need for biblical knowledge. Bible 101 offers a look at the big picture of the Bible and helps learners know how all of the passages fit into the whole biblical story. Within the context of the big picture, individual Bible stories have greater meaning and provide deeper growth in faith. The most knowledgeable Christian appreciates a review of the Bible; however, the very title suggests that this is a comfortable place for the beginner. Bible 101 may become the entry point for the new or renewed Christian, and it offers an understanding of the gospel message that every Christian can share with others.

This intensive Bible study is an essential part of the "being disciples" part of this year's theme. Discipleship includes knowing the story: the story of Jesus, the story of God's people, and the story of the church. Knowing the story is a big step toward telling the story and "making disciples."

2. Small-group opportunities. In smaller groups, Christians can nurture one another, find support and care, explore questions and issues, enjoy fellowship, and continue to grow in faith. Small groups provide an avenue for new members to become integrated into the life and care of the congregation. Some small groups already exist at Christ Church, and the plan is to establish new ones. Right now, this feels overwhelming to leaders, so they will take more time to implement this step. They scheduled one small group for mid-winter and secured a skilled leader.

In the coming months, several committees will consider possible small-group opportunities to initiate in the future. While everyone will be invited to a small-group seminar, several potential small-group leaders will be identified and recruited to attend and to continue in an eight-week leadership-training program to follow. That will set the stage for implementing the small-group opportunities that build on Bible 101.

During this discussion of small group opportunities, a synod staff person who offers training in Identifying Spiritual Gifts contacted the church, inquiring if there was interest in a visit. In the midst of the planning process, this unexpected resource caught the attention of church leaders. Small groups will provide an arena in which spiritual gifts might be identified and nurtured. The church council will take part in the first of several Spiritual Gifts seminars to happen this year. This is only one example of how, as one staff person says, "Things just seem to fall into place."

Small groups offer a place for "being disciples." In such groups, Christians explore, question, discuss, and discern what it means to live as Christians today. Living faithfully everyday is enhanced through the nurture of other Christians who also attempt to "be disciples" in daily life. The everyday business of being disciples is the Christian's greatest witness to faith. It is a powerful invitation for others to become disciples.

3. Learning to share the faith. The third piece of the "Being disciples, making disciples . . . the adventure begins" is a Lenten emphasis. Christ Church has a history of offering Lenten mid-week worship and education. This year's Lenten focus will be how God is working in each person's own life. It is an experience of telling one's faith story and sharing the experience of God acting in one's life. Pastor Tim previously used a resource that he will adapt for use in this congregation during Lent to help people become more comfortable in sharing their faith.

"Being disciples" includes telling the faith story in actions and in words. Small groups may be very effective in helping persons live their faith; however, many Christians are reluctant to speak of their faith to others. For some, it comes naturally; for others, it does not. This Lenten focus helps people recognize that they have a faith story and helps them put that faith story into words. It also reveals the many ways in which faith sharing can happen. Faith sharing is a step in "making disciples."

Pastor Tim and DCE Heidi call this year The Grand Experiment. It is an experiment in living out a vision statement: "Challenging Everyone to Experience an Adventurous Life with Christ Now." They say repeatedly, "We are not afraid of failing." They do not know where the year will lead, but there is a plan. The plan has been constructed in conversations among many church leaders, and the construction continues. Sometimes, new ideas fit into the existing plan, such as the offer of a Spiritual Gifts Seminar. Sometimes, new ideas require more discernment. Energy has been created as church leaders have met together around the new vision statement. So, the "grand experiment begins now. . . ."

What Is Going on Here?

In most congregations, there are natural cycles of vision and energy. Not content to continue their current "wilderness journey," Christ Church struggled to develop a new vision statement just as they called a new pastor, and the new pastor took seriously their stated vision. In fact, he used his own arrival to add momentum to the flicker of energy that had been created. Engaging congregational leaders, Pastor Tim and DCE Heidi fanned in to flame a plan that challenges this church to grow in discipleship. The plan, when viewed in a linear fashion, moves from Bible study, to small relational groups, to faith-sharing experiences. Such endeavors are not necessarily linear in an established church, but this plan provides a framework for both existing ministries and new ones as the church seeks to help members both be disciples and make disciples.

Other Stories of Education and Evangelism

Outreach, Education, and Special Needs. "It is the mission of Middleburg Early Education Center to serve children and families in a loving, Christian environment." For more than thirty years, Bethel Lutheran Church of Middleburg, Ohio, has reached out to young children in the name of Jesus. MEEC is a non-profit organization licensed by the Ohio Department of Human Services that provides preschool for typically developing children and early intervention and therapies for children with special needs. Without hesitation, MEEC announces that children will be served "in a loving, Christian environment." The staff of eighteen could be doing other things, but this is their way of responding to God's call in their lives. This ministry is a response to God's love, driven by the church's passion for Christ.

The sentence, "My child has special needs" brings together people of many cultures and religions. MEEC serves families that are Muslim and Hindu, as well as Christian. Every week Pastor Krebill visits the Center to read Bible stories and pray, and simply to live out the love of God.

"God's Faithful Followers" is a second ministry of Bethel that provides an environment for Christian education for adults with developmental disabilities. This ministry is ecumenical and open to all. Every Thursday evening, God's Faithful Followers provides worship, fellowship, caring Christian friends, an opportunity to learn about God, crafts to make and take, and, often, a brief respite for caregivers.

The Web site of Bethel Lutheran Church announces, "We firmly believe that coming together to study the Word of God, and to make connections between that Word and our lives is important to the ongoing discipleship of all Christians." That connection between God's Word and daily life is lived out in these two distinct ministries with those with disabilities and special needs, both children and adults. Is this Christian education? Absolutely. Children and adults are learning of Jesus in a developmentally appropriate manner. Is this evangelism? Absolutely. Children, adults, and families in the community of various faith traditions and cultures know that it is the love of Jesus Christ that is expressed in these ministries.

Center for Faith and Life. At the Lutheran Church of the Holy Spirit in Emmaus, Pennsylvania, the Web site says everything about education and evangelism: "Our mission is to equip the baptized for their ministry in the world, the community, the workplace, the home, and in the congregation. This ministry, through witness and service to others, empowered by the Holy Spirit, seeks to introduce others to Jesus Christ and thereby invite them into His Church. In Baptism they join us in commitment and mission." At Holy Spirit, the connection between faith and daily life is stated clearly and often: it is the connection between study and the life of discipleship that witnesses to the world.

Adult education is offered through the Center for Faith and Life. This very name emphasizes the vital connection between the life of faith and the life of discipleship. Adults are invited to explore Bible study, parent support, small-group ministry, book groups, new-member classes, and topical studies. Two offerings, however, focus on helping church members live faithfully everyday. One study continually asks, "How do I relate my faith to my occupation?" A second group discusses case studies with ethical dilemmas in the workplace.

Christian education usually takes one of two models: 1) students begin with Scripture or theology, then seek the implications for daily life, or 2) students begin with a question or problem from everyday, then seek the wisdom or guidance of Scripture or theological resources. Both models are offered at Holy Spirit, providing a variety of ways to connect study and the life of discipleship.

Special-occasion visitors. Many congregations usually have guests present where there is an affirmation of baptism or First Communion service. And there are visitors at Vacation Bible School and most special events. Church leaders experience the visitor at special occasions as a mixed blessing. There may be some resentment that persons attend only for the special occasions, not at other times. Like the prodigal son's older brother, some are there all the time, carrying the weight of responsibility, doing what needs to be done. Now a visitor shows up and gets lots of attention.

On the other hand, some people need a special reason to come to church. They simply are not going to walk in the door without an excuse. What better excuse for coming to the church than the First Communion, confirmation, or choir performance of a nephew, neighbor, grandchild, or daughter of a friend? Perhaps they will never come again. Perhaps they will find a welcome. Perhaps today is a moment of readiness to explore the church as part of their life.

Educational events provide unique opportunities for inviting others to join us in church. Few aspects of ministry offer so many occasions to say, "Please come along. We would love to have you."

A Ride to Church Can Change a Life. Today, Shari is a Lutheran pastor. When she was a kindergartner, her family was not active in church, but her Montessori school met in a church building. When her mom saw the vacation Bible school poster on the wall, she enrolled Shari for a week that summer, and Shari loved VBS. That is probably why she was excited the following year when two friends invited her to go with them to Sunday school and children's choir. First-graders invited a first-grade friend to join them at church! The friend's mom stopped to give Shari a ride each Sunday morning and, as the saying goes, the rest is history.

Shari thrived in church activities, especially education. She describes herself as "a pest in confirmation because I loved it so much." In church, she had found a special place where she was cherished and nurtured. Today, she is a pastor.

Years later, when talking with a search committee interviewing her as their pastor, she heard one woman talking about stopping each Sunday to give a young boy a ride to church. "That," Shari said, "was my own story. Someone gave me a ride every Sunday and it changed my life." Later that year, Pastor Shari baptized the young boy, now a confirmation student in that congregation.

What Can Be Learned from These Churches?

What can we learn from these congregations as they take seriously the call to educate and the call to evangelize? In reading these stories, the following learnings emerge (readers may draw further implications):

1. These congregations tailor their ministries. No two congregations go about evangelism and education in the same ways. They identify their community contexts, their moment in this congregation's ongoing life, the current strengths of the congregation, and the resources available to them.
2. There are some common components of education and evangelism among these congregations.
    a. A basic study of the Bible and the Christian faith is available, especially for those new to the church. Newcomers always have a place to begin, and long-time members have a place to refresh their knowledge.
    b. Growing in knowledge of the Bible and in an understanding of discipleship is encouraged. There are a variety of opportunities for continuing study, often including the use of small-group settings that encourage growth in discipleship.
    c. The daily lives of members are seen as the arena where faith is lived. Helping Christians connect faith and work, faith and home, faith and relationships is explicitly addressed in study and discussion groups.

d. Invitations and opportunities to visit, attend, and join this church are frequent and public. The congregations use special events, workplace conversations, neighborhood gatherings, and community outreach to invite others to come into the church building and participate in church activities.

3. Skill and comfort in talking about faith are not assumed. Many people, perhaps most, are shy about speaking of their church and their faith. These congregations help people find the words and the encouragement to tell others the good news of the gospel. Members learn when and how they can invite others to join them in this journey of faith. These learnings are scattered throughout education and congregational life, people's questions are explicitly addressed.

4. Commitment, enthusiasm, and thoughtful planning by pastor, staff, and church leaders may motivate and inspire others to take part in study and growth opportunities. There is an expectancy that people will participate. That participation may naturally lead to one-to-one witnessing and faith-sharing by Christians.

The connection between education and evangelism may be the most natural relationship in ministry. This chapter has illustrated how some churches have developed that partnership. These stories may offer some ideas, spark new ideas of your own, inspire you to take a new look at these ministries, and encourage you to consider the education-evangelism connection in your own church. We have a gospel to live and to share. Education and evangelism are instrumental in helping us do both.

Questions for Reflection and Conversation

1. When and how can a person learn the basics of the Bible and the Christian faith in your church?

2. In what ways are small groups used to encourage growth in discipleship in your church? What other opportunities challenge people to grow beyond the basics?

3. When and how are members encouraged to explore the concrete implications of faith as it is lived at work and home?

4. How do people in your surrounding community, visitors, and occasional attenders hear the invitation to come and join in church activities?

5. What is the relation between good planning and commitment? How can the enthusiasm of your church leaders be stimulated? What's holding you back?

Parish Strategies

1. Divide a gathering (committee, task force, etc.) into the following three groups:

   1) Learning the basics of Bible and faith

   2) Connecting faith and daily life

   3) Learning to talk about my faith

   Ask each group to list the current opportunities for this in the congregation, then list additional ways for this to happen.

2. Create a faith "question of the month" about which members may share; then invite that sharing at home and gatherings throughout the month. For example, "What is your favorite hymn?" "What is your first memory of going to church?"

Education and evangelism make wonderful partners

6. CHRISTIAN EDUCATION AS EVANGELISM IN A MULTICULTURAL SETTING

Eddie K. Kwok

Outside the Heritage Hall of Zion Lutheran Church in downtown Saskatoon, Saskatchewan, a dozen or so Chinese residents from the local community gather every Sunday morning at 10:00 A.M. The occasion is not a typical adult Sunday school. The Chinese are meeting for the purpose of learning English. Most of them are not members of Zion, a predominantly white congregation. In fact, most of them are not Christians. They are new immigrants from various provinces in China. Ron, a retired school principal who has taught English in the People's Republic of China, teaches one of the two classes. He is assisted by a couple of other people from the congregation. The group uses the lectionary readings and other material from the Christian tradition instead of the typical curriculum that one would expect for an English as a Second Language (ESL) class. After class, members of the group proceed into the Heritage Hall for a worship service conducted in Cantonese and Mandarin. During the week, the same group of people meets for a Bible study that is conducted in Mandarin at one of the members' homes.

The Church as Context for Learning English

Admittedly, providing language classes as a service to new immigrants is not a recent evangelism initiative. Historically, communities across Canada have recognized the important connection between language abilities and assimilation. Proficiency in the English language is a key criterion that most employers are looking for. The job market favors those who come from English-speaking countries. Immigrants from countries that speak other languages, no matter how experienced they were in their fields prior to coming to Canada, first have to overcome their deficit in the English language before they can expect to make their contributions with their specific work skills and experience.

Chinese immigrants, in particular, have always recognized the importance of learning English as a way of integrating into Canadian society. For most of them, it is a key element in the set of survival skills that will enable them to find their way around in their new surroundings. The flood of new immigrants who came to Canada from Hong Kong prior to 1997, the year the British handed over their former colony to the Chinese government, intensified the demand for community-based English classes. In the mid-1990s, many

Chinese communities across Canada, including Chinese congregations, responded to the need by organizing English classes for new immigrants. While most congregations recruited teachers from their own membership rolls, some hired professional English teachers for this purpose. Clearly, the hope of these Chinese congregations in offering English-language classes was that the new immigrants who came to these classes would be exposed to the gospel and respond in faith. However, while some newcomers do eventually become members of the congregation, many simply take advantage of the service and have nothing more to do with the church. As a result, many congregations have questioned whether or not this is a cost-effective way of reaching out to new immigrants.

From the point of view of many new Chinese immigrants, learning English in the context of the Christian tradition appears to be an acceptable option. Some of them see this purely as a form of social service provided by the church, and so they are there to take advantage of the opportunity. They do not stay for the worship service, but leave right after the class is over. Others, however, are curious about the church and are open to learning about Christianity. These are the ones who usually remain behind for the worship service. But personal agendas are not the only determinants of whether or not these new immigrants will eventually become members of the congregation. Other factors, such as the hospitality of the congregation, their sense of community, and eventually the establishment of relationships also play important roles. Most important, behind all of these human factors is the experience of hearing the gospel and encountering the living Christ.

Christian Education and the Challenge of Multiculturalism

Zion Lutheran Church is not the only congregation that has started offering English-language classes to new immigrants. Many others across Canada are developing similar programs. This initiative is one response by the church to address a greater challenge—the challenge of multiculturalism. Multiculturalism is being used in this chapter as a social phenomenon, rather than as an ideology. It is the coming together of many different people representing a diversity of ethnicity and culture. Defined this way, multiculturalism is a description of the social fabric of an increasing number of communities across North America.

The increasing diversity of our communities is evidenced in the growing number of restaurants serving ethnic food that may have seemed exotic a few years ago. It is now common for supermarkets to have an Asian section to cater to the growing demand of an expanding Asian community. The distinctive minaret of a mosque and the unique architecture of a Hindu, Sikh, or Buddhist temple is fast becoming part of the landscape of many Canadian communities. In metropolitan centers, such as Vancouver and Toronto, the people one meets are as likely to be Asian as they are of Eurpoean descent. Similarly, the languages spoken on the streets of these centers are just as likely to be Asian as English.

The changing demographic of our urban centers calls attention to the need for a different way of providing ministry. The traditional model of ministry that was based on gathering together immigrants from specific geographical areas in Europe no longer suffices in today's multicultural society. Since congregations were originally established along ethnic lines, the church has yet to fully learn how to minister cross-culturally. Similarly, mission developers were once trained to work within their own specific ethnic communities, but they were not equipped to deal with those coming from very different ethnic backgrounds. Even if they have the desire, people in many congregations do not have the necessary experience or skills for cross-cultural ministry. More important, congregations are recognizing that they require a whole new understanding of ministry and evangelism that is appropriate in the new context. Ministry in a multicultural setting calls for a very different approach and also a very different kind of leadership. Most of all, it calls for the renewal of the church to become truly the church in an increasingly globalized world. The task of Christian education then is to facilitate the church in its renewal. It is to assist the church in the reassessment of its own identity and its understanding of ministry and mission. It is also to design a comprehensive curriculum that can help to relocate the Christian faith from a parochial to a global context. ("Curriculum" here refers to the entire Christian education endeavor, not to curriculum resources). Another key task of Christian education is to provide resources and training materials so that the church can be equipped with knowledge and skills that will empower its members for cross-cultural ministry. With these tasks in mind, what shape does Christian education for evangelism in a multicultural setting take? What are some key aspects that should be included in the curriculum, and why are they so critical in helping the church develop a model of cross-cultural ministry?

Christian education in a multicultural setting calls for a globalized curriculum and an appropriate pedagogy in both context and ethos. A globalized curriculum means that the Christian faith is no longer taught only in the context of its own traditions, but in the context of other religions as well. In other words, the context is no longer the North American, white, middle-class community. The context is the world community and the multicultural matrix of the local community. The stories, songs, and illustrations used in teaching materials must be drawn from the global community. A globalized curriculum also calls for a new hermeneutic. Biblical texts are no longer interpreted only from a Western perspective, but now include perspectives from other parts of the world. Learning to read the Bible with developing-world eyes cannot only help the reader gain insights that are normally hidden from a monocultural reading; it can also help the reader appreciate the richness of other cultures and their contributions to the Christian church.

Teaching the Christian Faith in the Context of World Religions

A key aspect of the content of a globalized curriculum is that the Christian faith is taught in the context of other religions. We typically read the Bible, creeds, and confessions, asking only what their content means for us *in* the church. As such, we seek to discover the relevancy for ourselves without bothering to figure out its significance for members of our community who do not share our faith. While an introspective study of the Christian faith may enhance and deepen our understanding of texts, it does little to help us understand ourselves better as Christians and as a church in relation to the wider community. Clearly, this is one reason why, as a church, we are experiencing difficulties in relating to people of other faiths and doing evangelism.

The reality of religious pluralism that the church has found so troubling is not a new phenomenon. Reading the Old Testament reminds us that the faith of the people of God was lived out long ago in the midst of a plurality of religions. The story of the Old Testament is, in part, a story of how the faith of the Hebrew people was shaped and transformed through its interaction with various ancient Near Eastern religions. The biblical texts clearly chronicle how the Hebrew people resisted and, on many occasions, succumbed to the adulteration of their religious tradition as they dwelled alongside other Canaanite communities. At the same time, the biblical texts also show evidence of extensive sharing of material, in form and content, with other ancient Near Eastern cultures. The faith of the Hebrew people did not come to us in a pristine form, preserved from the very beginning, but in a form that resulted from a dynamic interaction with neighboring religious faiths. In that process, the Hebrews' faith and religious traditions were profoundly shaped and enriched.

The same phenomenon is presented to us in the New Testament, where the gospel is proclaimed in a world that is no less diverse than what we have now. Jesus did not intend for his disciples to keep the gospel strictly as a Jewish cult. If that was to have been the case, then we would not have the church. Instead, he sent his disciples out to proclaim the good news everywhere. In the process, the gospel was shaped through its interaction with the many different cultures that it encountered. While the essential message remained unchanged, Jesus was presented differently in different contexts in order that the good news might be heard. The early Christian church in Jerusalem had to deal with divisive issues that came with Gentile conversion, such as circumcision and the meat of strangled animals (Acts 15). The apostle Paul, too, had to resolve the controversy regarding the eating of food sacrificed to idols in the Corinthian church (1 Corinthians 8). Difficult, divisive issues face the Church also in today's pluralistic context.

Pluralism need not be a reality to be feared. In fact, it can be seen as a friend—a gift from God to the church. Pluralism forces us to ask some difficult questions that we otherwise may never ask. The plurality of religions and the uniqueness of Christ is one question that will not easily go away. Neither should it be one that the church avoids. It is when the church grapples with such difficult questions that it will discover more about itself and its mission, about evangelism and education. Learning about other religions helps us to understand how they are different from and similar to Christianity. It forces us to ask why we believe what we believe. It leads us to redefine our identity as Christians and to examine what it means to be witnesses in a world that we share with other faiths.

Teaching the Christian faith in the context of other religions can facilitate members in their conversations with people of other faiths. The media can be helpful in making us more aware of other cultures and religions. The Discovery Channel and National Geographic often offer insights that raise our level of consciousness to the diversity within our own communities. The content of these programs can serve as the bases for discussions and conversations. Actual visits to the places of worship of other faith traditions can help congregation members better understand the background of people who live in their community. Moreover, inviting members of other religious traditions into the church for conversations can greatly enhance our understanding of these traditions. Conversely, members of the church may be invited by other religious traditions to make presentations of the Christian faith.

Such gestures provide opportunities for interfaith conversations that serve to promote a deeper understanding of one another's religious beliefs. Most of all, they can help put a familiar human face on a generic textbook or media presentation of facts and information. Various opportunities for learning about other religious traditions often present themselves in our communities. These include invitations to collaborate in social and community welfare programs, national and global disaster-relief projects, and religious forums and dialogues.

Teaching Hospitality

We live in the midst of a climate of suspicion. Some people may be afraid of people who come from places that have been associated with terrorism. We teach our children not to trust strangers. Yet, I can still remember a song that I was taught to sing when I was very young. It goes like this:

> A visitor came to see my father
> But my father was not home.
> I invited the visitor to come in, have a seat,
> And offered the visitor a cup of tea.

Clearly, encouraging a child to invite a stranger into the home when the parents are not present would be inconceivable in today's society here in North America, but as a child I was taught to welcome the visitor.

So what is hospitality? What is it today, particularly in a fearful society? It is much deeper than any one action alone. It is to create space for others, to share our space with them. It is to make room so that the other person can experience the same freedoms, rights, and benefits that we have. Hospitality is deeply rooted in culture. Every culture has its own way of expressing hospitality. But hospitality does not mean imposing our cultural values on others, or thinking that our culture is superior to others'. It is to treat others with respect and honor as we would like to be respected and honored. Hospitality has no room for racism.

More than just cultural practice, hospitality is also a key theological theme that runs through both the Old and New Testaments. God is portrayed as a God of hospitality. Beginning with the creation accounts, we are told that it was God who planted the Garden of Eden and placed the first human beings there. God not only created the first man and woman, God also created a "hospitable" space for them. God provided "space" for Abraham and his descendents as they made their journey from one place to another. Those who welcomed them were blessed, while those who were inhospitable suffered consequences. Hospitality was written into the statues of the Israelite society when they finally settled into the land that was promised to them through Abraham. The Israelites were called to be hospitable to the sojourners and aliens who lived among them. The law provided for these groups of people, considered to be migrants in our present-day language. They were permitted to glean in the fields after the harvest was done.

The theme of hospitality continues in the New Testament, and takes on a more defined, theological and Christological emphasis. God's hospitality is revealed in the good news of the Kingdom of God and is extended to all alike. Yet, it is also clear that not everyone is appreciative of God's hospitality. The religiously and materially self-sufficient were portrayed as those who rejected God's hospitality. The prostitutes, publicans, and tax collectors, on the other hand, were singled out as the subjects through whom Jesus demonstrated the hospitality of God. Hospitality to the marginalized, such as the widows, the Samaritans, and the poor, became important issues in the Gospels, particularly in Luke. When the king's invitation in the Parable of the Wedding Banquet was spurned by the guests, he invited those on the highways and the byways—strangers. As these strangers accepted the king's invitation and savoured the banquet prepared for them, they were transformed. They were no longer strangers, but friends.

Conversely, inhospitality is perceived in the Bible as a grave sin that is often punished with immediate consequences. As mentioned above, in the Pentateuch, those who extended hospitality to the people of God were blessed, whereas those who were inhospitable, experienced God's judgment. Some have interpreted the destruction of Sodom as judgment for their sins of inhospitality. Inhospitality in the New Testament takes the form of religious exclusivism. Jesus criticized the religious leaders of the day for "keeping people out of the kingdom of God." Paul fought tirelessly against an exclusivistic Jewish mindset that was limiting people of other cultures from hearing the gospel—the same mindset that also sought to impose its own culture on others as a condition for the gospel.

In our present context, congregations have generally adopted a form of hospitality that they extend to those who come into the church on Sunday morning. Essentially, it includes the following welcoming gestures:

- Welcome at the entrance of the church by ushers
- Introduction before the service, during announcements, or at the end of the service
- Welcome to coffee hour after the service by members of the congregation

- Visitation by pastor or pastoral team members
- Invitation to participate in other church activities such as Bible studies, women's, or youth groups

Typically, the kind of hospitality practiced by the church is limited to newcomers who step into the church. The implication is that hospitality tends to be territorial—it is limited to the confines of the church building or the membership roll of the congregation. The biblical concept of hospitality, however, goes far beyond this normal practice. Hospitality is extended beyond the physical boundaries of the church and members of the congregation. The wider community, even the global community, is to be the recipient of a congregation's hospitality. This is hospitable evangelism.

It is not as if the church is unaware of its social responsibilities in the world. The call to be a welcoming church is clearly written in the policies of the church, and congregations are encouraged to put them into practice. But policies are not always translated into practice. Some congregations practice hospitality by being involved in cross-cultural ministries, such as refugee sponsorship programs. These efforts, however, are mostly initiated by individuals or small groups within the congregation. Clearly, hospitality has to be more than rhetoric and policies. Otherwise, the evangelical practice of hospitality will continue to be sporadic and piecemeal. Intentionality is a critical factor in the cultivation of a culture of hospitality. Members of the congregation have to desire to be more hospitable. Welcoming newcomers into our community must be a key theme in the curricula of Christian education in order to inform and encourage every member in the congregation, whether young or old, to participate in the creation of a tradition of hospitality.

It is clear that hospitality is a key theme for Christian education in a multicultural setting. Curriculum endeavors have to be designed to help congregations become hospitable communities where newcomers feel welcomed. What a wonderful opportunity to explain why we believe what we believe! Is it not a great privilege to be able to explain to someone why our church worships God in a particular way? Is this not what the apostle Paul tells his readers when he writes to them that they should be prepared in season and out of season to give an account of their faith? Is this Christian education? Definitely! Is this evangelism? Most certainly!

Teaching Community

Clearly, one cannot speak of human relationships in the church apart from the experience of *koinonia*. The church has always taught that all human relationships are founded on the divine-human relationship. Reconciliation with God makes possible reconciliation with other people. Lutherans have emphasized the need for the justified to live out their justification in their communities. Our being and our behaviors are grounded in the person and works of Jesus Christ. We believe that our faith in Jesus Christ is the center out of which everything else proceeds, including *koinonia*. For someone who comes into the church from outside of the Christian tradition, the movement may well be in the opposite direction. Many have come to faith in Jesus Christ through the experience of *koinonia*. Let me illustrate this point with an example.

Many years ago, a group of Christians studying at a university met regularly for Bible studies every week. Outside of these meetings, they also did many things as a group and often had meals together. It was not an exclusive community. Other students, including non-Christians, were welcomed to participate and to be part of the group. In time, the group became larger and larger, as more and more students joined the group. What is even more significant is that many of those who joined the group as non-Christians eventually became Christians as a result of their experience of community. I was one of them.

For the Chinese, a sense of community is as vital to their well-being as are their jobs and their families. This sense of community is often expressed by the frequent potluck dinners that have become a trademark of Chinese congregations. Members of Chinese congregations often have lunch together after worship service on Sundays. In a way, one can say that, for Chinese congregations, communion begins at the table and does not end with the post-communion blessing, but continues even after the sending. Whether the setting is a Chinese dim-sum restaurant or a potluck, the celebration of God's hospitality continues, albeit in a less formal way. In another sense, one can also say that, for Chinese congregations, the response to "go in peace and serve the Lord" does not stop with a verbal expression of gratitude to God for the gifts of peace and ministry. It is also expressed in the *koinonia* that is experienced in the meal that they have together.

Obstacles and Challenges

Cultivating a culture of hospitality in congregations is not without obstacles. Some of these obstacles have little to do with cultural differences between existing members of the congregation and newcomers, but are existing aspects of the congregation's culture. Every congregation already has its own distinctive culture. One can speak of a congregational culture as being warm or cool; vibrant or sluggish; open or closed. Congregational culture reflects the outlook of its members, particularly the dominant ones who are often in leadership. Of course, congregations, like any other community, are not without their own prejudices and ignorance. Not everyone in the congregation has had the experience of being acquainted with, or even wants to be with, people of other cultures. Generally, ignorance can be addressed by providing information and opportunities to meet people of other races, ethnicities, and cultures. Prejudices are much harder to deal with. Attitudinal change takes time. Christian education in a multicultural setting program cannot be limited to occasional and isolated teaching of cultural issues. Cultivating a climate of hospitality requires an extensive Christian education program that provides both resources and experiences aimed at informing and transforming members of the congregation. Hopefully, as members of the congregation become more acquainted with people from other cultures, they will become more open and accepting.

Congregations sometimes lapse into states of complacency. When they do, they tend to be more concerned with maintaining the status quo than with reaching out to those who are new in the community. Caught in a mode where members are mainly interested in their own welfare, these congregations have little desire for change. For this reason, they make little or no effort to welcome newcomers. Sharing space with these strangers often means having to make adjustments in one's own life and lifestyle. Hospitality carries with it a certain degree of vulnerability that many are not prepared to risk. On the other hand, a congregation with declining membership may be prepared to take the risk out of a sense of desperation. However, hospitality that is crisis-driven is not really hospitality. Typically, members of a congregation that find themselves in such a situation are primarily interested in their own survival as a congregation. The hospitality that they practice tends to be self-directed and, therefore, unhealthy. Newcomers are perceived as assets that can help turn their situation around. Evangelism and the mission of the church then become equated with increasing membership to save a dying congregation.

The fear of change that is often manifested in congregations can be indicative of broader problems. Confronted with the reality of declining membership and benevolence, mainline denominations feel the need to expand their ecclesiastical and missional horizons and to pay serious attention to demographic shifts and immigration patterns across the country. Congregations are beginning to look into establishing cross-cultural ministries, but their efforts are often hampered by a lack of resources and expertise in this area. Generally, congregations are not familiar with relating to people coming from different cultural backgrounds. Moreover, their understanding of ministry among people of different cultures is often limited to secondhand information communicated to them through experiences of missionaries overseas. It is one thing to hear about people of other ethnic or cultural backgrounds. It is another to actually live in close proximity to them or share the same roof. Uncomfortable as the experience may be, it does serve as a reminder that mission and evangelism are not only the responsibility of missionaries that we send overseas, but is the calling that every member of the church is asked to undertake.

Christian education clearly will have to be carried out from a global context in order to facilitate congregations in developing some degree of cultural savvy that is essential for multicultural ministry. Congregations would do well to include in their curriculum classes, such as: Introduction to World Religions; Racism; Cultural Anthropology; Intercultural Communication. Of course, there is no substitute for the experience of listening and learning from those in our neighborhoods who are of a different faith or from a different culture. Too often, the church becomes so preoccupied with internal problems that it no longer has the time or resources to help congregations become equipped for mission in today's multicultural society.

Cultural barriers exist between ethnic groups in communities, even though they are often not visible until there is a conflict. They remain one of the key obstacles that a congregation will face in the establishment of cross-cultural ministry. For this reason, a key learning objective of Christian education in a multicultural setting is to seek to bridge the cultural gap that exists between newcomers and existing members of a congregation. Of course, barriers already exist among different ethnic or language groups, even within congregations. For instance, even within a Chinese-Lutheran congregation in Canada, it is not unusual to find a number of distinct language subgroups. The Chinese immigrants from Hong Kong speak Cantonese, but not Mandarin. Those from mainland China speak Mandarin, but not Cantonese. Culturally, there is a huge gap between the two groups of immigrants. Immigrants from Taiwan speak Mandarin, but culturally and politically, they are distinct from those from mainland China, even though the two share the same language. To complicate matters further, there is another subgroup of immigrants from Malaysia who speak Hakka. Finally, one also has to consider the second generation—those who are born or raised in Canada and who may speak only English. To a non-Chinese person looking at a congregation from the outside, the distinction among these subgroups is not apparent. Nevertheless, congregations desiring to establish cross-cultural ministry would do well to become familiar with the diversity that exists among those of the same ethnicity. The task of educating congregations for cross-cultural ministry has to be part of an overall, sustained effort by the church to educate its members and equip them for ministry in a rapidly changing world.

As formidable as cultural differences may seem, they can be bridged. Congregations can learn about these differences and how to handle them. Newcomers to the church often bring with them customs and practices that may seem strange and even shocking to members of a congregation. Often, the temptation is for the congregation to make newcomers conform to the status quo behavior. Such an assimilation model of multicultural ministry not only generates conflicts, but also deprives the congregation of the experience of learning from another culture. It robs the congregation of the opportunity to rediscover their faith by looking at it from a different cultural perspective.

Clearly, one of the most important tasks of Christian education and evangelism in a multicultural setting is to promote understanding among the different cultural groups represented in the congregation and the community. While formal learning settings such as in-house presentations, can be useful, members of the congregation learn best when they are exposed to cultural events where they can experience the various aspects of another culture and begin to appreciate its richness. The goal is to allow the different cultural groups represented in the congregation to become familiar with other customs and practices. It helps members of the congregation discover the significance behind various cultural traditions. Monthly potluck meals comprised of a variety of cuisines representing the diversity in the congregation are usually well received. Festive events, such as Chinese New Year and Mid-Autumn Festival, are ideal occasions for members of a congregation to learn about another culture. Joint services that offer a liturgy in different languages can help foster a sense of community in diversity. Conversely, Thanksgiving, Christmas, Good Friday, and Easter are excellent opportunities for inviting the community to learn about the Christian tradition. Congregations must intentionally plan for these events and encourage members to attend.

Congregations need to be transformed in order to provide effective evangelism in a multicultural setting. The task of Christian education is to facilitate the church in its renewal with the gifts that God has already brought into their communities. These are the strangers living in their midst. It is with the help of these strangers that the church can rediscover its identity and mission. As the church shares its own gifts with the strangers, and the strangers with the church, strangers become friends and the gospel of Jesus Christ is embodied and articulated in a new and living way that gives life to all in the community.

Questions for Reflection and Conversation

1. Who are the strangers in your community? How are people in your congregation just as strange to them? How might each learn about the other?

2. What are some ways your congregation offers hospitality? How might those be expanded and deepened in order to create a tradition of broad hospitality beyond the church doors and the present membership?

3. What are some specific biblical stories that might help various age groups in your congregation learn more about God's call to be a hospitable people?

4. How might educational ministry in your congregation have a global perspective?

Parish Strategies

1. Explore places in your community where different racial or ethnic groups meet. With other leaders, develop some mutual learning experiences where people might talk with one another across multicultural divides. Out of these experiences, try to establish some sustained conversations and relationships where people might share what they believe and why.

Most importantly, behind all human factors, is the experience of hearing the gospel and encountering the living Christ.

7. REACHING OUT THROUGH LUTHERAN SCHOOLS

Nelson T. Strobert

My first encounter with Lutheran schools occurred while growing up in Brooklyn, New York, where I was nurtured in the faith by my parents, extended family, and the members of the Evangelical Lutheran Church of the Epiphany. The educational ministry program was comprehensive and pervaded the life of the congregation: Sunday school, confirmation classes, and at various times, vacation church school. In addition, there was (and continues to be) the parochial school with students from pre-K through eighth grade. I can still recall the first graduation at the school where my friends and I served as acolytes at worship. There was one graduate that first year.

As the years passed, students came from within the congregation as well as from various parts of the borough of Brooklyn. Not all of the children in the parochial school were members of Epiphany, but membership and worship participation in a congregation was expected. As part of the curriculum, students attended chapel on Wednesday morning. Years later, after seminary, when I came home to visit my family, I would attend the weekday worship at Epiphany with the school children. Sometimes I presided and preached at chapel. It was not surprising to see, not only the students and the teachers, but also members of the congregation attending the weekday liturgy as part of their worship life. Some worshiped at that time because of Sunday work schedules. The tradition of this Lutheran school serving as a strong arm of education, worship, and outreach continues to this day, with the school shortly approaching fifty years of existence.

My second encounter with Lutheran schools occurred when I was a seminarian. I was a vicar/intern at Lord God of Sabaoth Lutheran Church on St. Croix in the U.S. Virgin Islands. One of the unique features of the parish at that time was the Lutheran kindergarten, which had been in the parish for over seventy years. It was interesting to watch the various young people come to the school each morning: a little United Nations with Cruzian (natives of St. Croix), continentals (from the mainland United States, black and white), down islanders (from islands in the southern Caribbean), and Asians. They would come in with smiling faces, talking with each other as they entered the courtyard of the parish hall, where the classrooms were located. As the day progressed, one could hear students singing, praying, reciting, and learning to live with each other in the classroom as well as in the open play area.

I enjoyed chapel conversations with these young people, playing guitar, singing church and folk hymns with them, and sharing some of the great stories from the Bible. They were curious and excited and reflective on what they had heard.

My third encounter with Lutheran parochial education occurred while I served as a parish pastor at Advent Lutheran Church in Cleveland, Ohio, that was a member of the Cleveland Urban Lutheran School. It was a cooperative venture among several churches representing what were then the three main Lutheran bodies in the city (the former American Lutheran Church, Lutheran Church in America, and the Lutheran Church-Missouri Synod). The children came from the contributing parishes as well as other denominations. Black and white students were studying, playing, and worshipping together. Teachers were certainly not on the same pay scale as their public-school counterparts, but certainly as well prepared in engaging these young students in their general and religious education.

Due to a lack of personnel one semester, I and several pastors were asked to teach one of the religion courses at the Lutheran high school on the east side of the city. It was a good opportunity for me to see directly what students were like in classroom interaction. I also served as an occasional chapel leader. Some students from my congregation attended there.

These four, brief scenarios show unique possibilities for students to encounter their peers, their teachers, and the church. These students were not all members of the sponsoring church or churches, they were not of one socioeconomic segment of the society, and they were not all Lutheran; however all shared in the educational mission of instruction in faith where students learn the good news of God's graciousness for all humankind. These were visible reminders of how cross-cultural and nonthreatening our congregations can be. One important piece of the educational ventures of congregations and associations of congregations involved in Lutheran early childhood and elementary education is the possibility of evangelism. Lutheran schools can and do reach out to others.

The Role of Lutheran Day Schools

Lutheran day schools predate the modern public school system.[1] As early as the mid-1600s in the mid-Atlantic region of the United States and stretching to the areas of the Midwest, Lutherans were concerned about and involved in the education of the young people. Presently there are over two thousand early childhood centers, two hundred elementary schools, and twenty high schools in the Evangelical Lutheran Church in America (ELCA). Building on the seminal educational works of Martin Luther, particularly *The Small Catechism* and the two treatises: "To the Councilmen of All Cities in Germany that They Establish and Maintain Christian Schools" and "A Sermon on Keeping Children in School," Lutheran churches have attempted to inculcate the educational tradition in the next generation of citizens for good citizenship, good government, and educated clergy; an education for service to God, the neighbor, and society at large.[2]

Here the word *education* is used very broadly to mean "the deliberate, systematic, and sustained effort to transmit, evoke, or acquire knowledge, values, attitudes, skills, or sensibilities, as well as any learning that results from the effort, direct or indirect, intended or unintended."[3] It is the intentional ways in which schools, agencies, Sunday schools, and so on, transmit the religious and cultural tradition. A part of education is an interpretive task; that is, assisting students to reflect and interpret their lives around the event of Jesus. While this happens in various ways, it is also done within the formal, implicit, and extracurricular activities within the Lutheran educational system. Lutheran schools are concerned about the general education of their students, and part of that general education is the tradition of the church and the Word of God in the Bible, Eucharist, and preaching. Many who come to the schools are Christian in background, but what might be the role of the early childhood center or day school within the general community? It is the same: a commitment to share the gospel story of Jesus with students who might be hearing it for the first time. This is evangelization.

Lutheran schools have attracted students whose families are new to the faith or are restoring their relationship with communities of faith. With the term *evangelization* one has the sense of actively telling the good news of Jesus to those who have not heard of God's gracious action for humankind. It is to tell the stories so that people who hear can, in turn, become disciples and share the story as well. Evangelization is rooted in the beginning of the Christian story. Examining the biblical texts in Acts 2:37-42 and Acts 4:1-4, we see the power that takes place with the preaching and teaching of the Word of God. In response to Peter's preaching, people were baptized, continued to study, and celebrated within the fellowship community. As Peter and John were teaching about Jesus, who rose from the dead, people heard the promise of God and believed what they had heard. We see the impact of the preaching and teaching; it meant growth in the community.

When some parents who have not been previously involved in communities of faith come to early childhood centers or schools, they often become engaged in the life of the Lutheran congregation or other congregations. It is with this understanding that the Lutheran educational system is part of the evangelization process of the church, as it is so succinctly stated, "an evangelizing church puts an evangelical imagination at the center of all its activities. Thus, the gospel witness becomes core to the entire life of the congregation and does not just function as a peripheral or programmatic activity."[4]

The Wisdom of School Administrators and Pastors

Lutheran schools can and do reach out to others. Many pastors and school administrators see evangelization as part of the educational endeavor of the church. What specifically might they mean by evangelization or evangelism in relation to these schools? How do they define the term? When asked, some of them said:

- "Reaching out to people who don't know Jesus; reaching out of your comfort zone to let God use you with neighbors."
- "The great commission; go spread the word."

- "Planting the seeds for the Holy Spirit. I think our calling is to expose children to the message of salvation."
- "Teaching. I always go back to 'Go ye. . . .' Sharing the Gospel through the spoken word; written word; good books; radio broadcasts. It should be personal."
- "To tell; like the angels; we are the ELCA, and Evangelical is in our name."
- "Christian friendship, which is journeying together with each other."
- "Presence, being relational . . . reaching out into the community, neighborhood, to whomever is present to say that there is a saving God; you have a reason for living; ministry in daily life."

Evangelism or evangelization is grounded in telling and sharing the Word of God, and yet it is still more. The school administrators and pastors were very cognizant of the communal components of this area of ministry, using words such as sharing, friendship, relationship, reaching out, responding to the great commission. These are all very active descriptors for the task. While the Word is shared in individual encounters in evangelism, these encounters lead individuals and students to life within the community of faith. Education is an opportunity to invite people into evangelical friendship and conversation. Through study, prayer, and worship, the Word of God continues to be shared. Lutheran schools can be a pivotal place for evangelization of the young as well as their families.

Voices of Teachers, Administrators, and Pastors on Evangelization

In preparation for this chapter, Donna Braband, the Director of Schools, ELCA, was asked her thoughts on the role of seminaries in relation to Lutheran schools and early childhood centers. In turn, she shared that question with pastors and administrative colleagues involved in ELCA schools.[5] Several of respondents talked about the need for future pastors and educators to know about and be skilled in evangelism, as they saw the schools as agents of evangelization.

If evangelism is a part of the Lutheran school and early-childhood-center experience, how is it demonstrated within the framework of these schools? ELCA and other Lutheran school pastors, teachers, and administrators, gave a broad range of possibilities:

Andrea Olson is a third grade teacher at Heritage Academy, a school of Association of Free Lutheran Churches (AFLC) in Maple Grove, Minnesota. She felt that evangelism had a definite place in the child's experience in the Lutheran school environment from the very beginning of the admission process. Questions are directed to the parents in terms of the expectations of the school. Olson was cognizant of the fact that not all children come from Christian homes where faith is nurtured. She feels that the evangelization process takes place within her classroom where she attempts to be sensitive to each of her students, as well as to personalize the relationship between herself and her students, "student by student."

The aspect of sharing was important to David Simpson in his description of evangelism. In his work as Director of Christian Education at Trinity Lutheran Church in Joppa, Maryland, Simpson felt that the sharing of self and the good news gave young people a foundation of faith. Since the school was open to everyone, many people became members of the church because of the outreach by the school and the invitation to parents to attend the special events in the school and the church.

Beverly Enderlein recently retired as administrator of the Heritage Academy of the AFLC in Maple Grove, Minnesota. She felt that outreach is an ideal goal, but also said that one has to be attentive to the context. In terms of the relationship to the sponsoring church, the board decided that they would not admit students whose families were not already active within their respective congregations. They wanted a commitment to Jesus Christ. While they could have had large numbers from the very beginning of the school project, their concern was not only strong academics but strong academics with strong religious education curriculum. In another context, she said (relating information from colleagues and friends in Minneapolis), a school was started, and evangelism was an important factor. Her feelings were that, what went on within the classroom prepared students to do evangelism outside the context of the school.

The Lutheran school is a strong place for evangelism, according to Jean Warfield, who had been the pastor of Bethany Lutheran Church and Leif Eriksson Lutheran School in Brooklyn, New York. She contends that the Lutheran school is a place where students can live and breathe the gospel in ways in which the worshipping congregation alone would not be able to help them do. The school is a safe place for those who would not otherwise come through the church door. In this place, the pastor also can help construct an environment that is Christ-based. She also emphasized the important role of the Lutheran identity in the school.

Discipleship is a key issue for Robert Gahagen, pastor of Epiphany Lutheran Church and School in Brooklyn, New York. Education is important for preparing disciples. Gahagen wants them to find their purpose in life, and for this, he believes, a Christian education is important. If they find that a family is not part of a faith community, they will invite them to the congregation. But in general, he feels this is a difficult task.

Paul Buchheimer, the headmaster of Advent Lutheran School in Boca Raton, Florida, finds that, for the large numbers of people (around one thousand including parents and students) who come through the entrance of the school each day, most bypass the doors of the church. The challenge for him is to be able to encourage them to consider visiting. For him, if the number-one purpose is not to bring children and families to God, then there really is no reason for a Lutheran school. They are not called to be a private school.

At Good Shepherd Lutheran Preschool in Fox Chapel, Pennsylvania, evangelism is described as "availability" to the parents. While the preschool is a service to the general community, the teachers will teach these toddlers various prayers as well as how to say grace. Pastor Robert Musser will readily send invitations to parents in the same envelope in which they receive the tuition payment notice. One example is an invitation for the children to bring their pets for the blessing of the animals. The director of the center attempts to complement the activities of the church with the center; the center also will have joint programs with the church, for example, food for the hungry.

Sarah Barrington, the administrator at Epiphany Lutheran School in Brooklyn, New York, states that the students spend a number of hours in the church as well as in the school. There is a strong need to educate the parents, Barrington believes, but this happens through the involvement of the parents in such things as school committees, potluck suppers, and house meetings. One child in this school, which requires church attendance, was sick one day and was not going be able to attend the Sunday liturgy. It was really important to him, so he asked his parent to take his place that Sunday. This demonstrates the power and influence of evangelization even with the youngest.

In the development of the Saint James Lutheran early childhood center in Gettysburg, Pennsylvania, evangelism, in the narrow sense of that word, was not a primary consideration. Fritz Foltz and Edward Keyser, retired pastors of the congregation, and Jamie Schaffer, a parishioner and one of the parents who spearheaded the formation of the center, noted that it was designed to provide a service to the community, particularly for children in households where there was only one parent, children from low-income families, special needs children, and infants. This is evangelization is the broad sense of the word. The chapel services have become the approach for education, but the fear of some of the directors of the center was that they were going to make "little Lutherans" of these youngsters. Chapel is important for sharing the good news with these children. The goal is not necessarily for them or their parents to become a part of the denomination.

The importance of chapel was also noted by Patricia Payne, a senior seminarian who was an intern at Phinney Ridge Lutheran Church in Seattle, Washington. She noted that chapel for the Child Development Center incorporated music and symbols of the church, which was met with enthusiasm and awe by the children.

Foundations in the Lutheran Tradition

There is no one method or fixed formula for sharing the good news of Jesus with families who are not presently involved in a faith community. Whereas some schools will require prior membership in a congregation as a criterion in the admissions process, others use the inactiveness or nonmembership of the parents as an opportunity for the evangelization process. In both venues, the concern is for relationship-building, which hopefully will be demonstrated within the school as well as beyond the walls of the school. The care and concern that are shown by teachers to students and parents and by administrators to staff, students, and families are the building blocks for vibrant Lutheran schools and early childhood education centers. The mutual conversation becomes the modus operandi for the Lutheran school. It is the gospel that is the center for all that takes place in the educational environment.

This builds on what is stated in the Smalkald Articles on the gospel:

We now want to return to the gospel, which gives guidance and help against sin in more than one way, because God is extravagantly rich in his grace: first, through the spoken word, in which the forgiveness of sins is preached to the whole world (which is the proper function of the gospel); second, through baptism; third, through the holy Sacrament of the Altar; fourth, through the power of the keys and also through the mutual conversation and consolation of brothers and sisters.[128] Matthew 18[:20*]: "Where two or three are gathered . . ."[6]

Some parents and children may hear the words of God's love, concern, and commitment to humankind for the first time; others may encounter the gospel in a fresh, new way. Hearing these words in various ways helps parents to know that they are not alone in the care and nurturing of their children. This may not be new for those who have been raised and nurtured in the church, but it can certainly be a welcome and supportive word to many who are struggling to be good parents in communities and a world that brings so much anxiety to daily life. A strong evangelizing word is also a reminder of God's unconditional love to those who have long been immersed in the life of the church.

The commitment to center the educational task in the gospel means that the faculty and staff must have a love for and commitment to the traditions of the church. One of the distinguishing features for Lutheran schools and early childhood centers is a respect for the Lutheran church tradition. Not all teachers in this area of educational ministry are members of the Lutheran church, but they need to be consciously supportive of the Lutheran educational task.

Born and raised in Guyana, Sarah Barrington has long been a Lutheran teacher and, for the past fifteen years, has been involved in administration at Epiphany Lutheran School. When she described her formation as a Lutheran school educator, she remembered being nurtured in the church: Sunday school student and teacher, Sunday school superintendent, special church assignments, and training in Lutheran schools and agencies of the church. All of these helped her to know and to be able to articulate Lutheran doctrine and tradition.

David Simpson, a senior seminarian at the time of this writing, was a director of Christian education at Trinity Lutheran Church and school in Joppa, Maryland, where he taught religious education in the middle school. While formally educated as a teacher, his work in Lutheran Christian education was rooted in quality classes offered by the pastor of the congregation, self-study, and conversations with the pastor. That helped him to know and appreciate the Lutheran theological tradition.

Paul Buchheimer grew up in the church with a father and grandfather who were pastors in the Lutheran Church Missouri Synod. He was educated at a church-related college. For him, it is important that the school assist in bringing children to Jesus Christ. Buchheimer feels that it is not the purpose of the Lutheran school to make these children Lutheran, but that the school use Lutheran doctrine as a means to assist in evangelization.

Each of these teachers and administrations in Lutheran schools is grounded in the Lutheran tradition. Their commitment is not only articulated, but demonstrated in how they interact with their students, colleagues, and parents in the classroom, in meetings, and in informal conversations.

Schools and Pastoral Leadership

What is the role of the pastor in Lutheran early childhood and elementary education? It is difficult to find pastoral candidates who want to be called to congregations where there is this educational component to the church's ministry.[7] As a teaching theologian in an ELCA seminary, I am particularly concerned about the way in which candidates for rostered ministry are prepared to work in such congregations. Those teaching at seminaries can learn from the concerns of pastors, teachers, and administrators of early childhood centers and schools.

Some pastors say that it is important to keep the faculty, staff, and congregation focused on what is really important in this area of the church's ministry. That means that the pastor has to be constantly appraised as to what the teachers and the administration in the school are doing. Just as important as oversight is inspiration for the personnel through the preached Word. For Pastor Gahagen, it is at chapel time where there are those teaching moments for faculty, staff, and students. Pastor Warfield feels that a pastor should not be only in the chapel, but everywhere. But this presence should be done unobtrusively, graciously, and wisely. For her, this means being present to staff, leadership, parents, and students. The key word for her is "missional." The pastor can help the staff see the gifts that they have and assist them in using those gifts in the ministry of the church. The pastor also helps to set the tone for the school and church. When this doesn't occur, there can be difficulty for all. Where the pastor is positively and integrally involved in the ministry of the school there is a ripple effect in the expansion of pastoral care beyond the walls of the congregation.

Pastors Fritz Foltz and Edward Kyser were involved in the formation of the childcare center at Saint James in Gettysburg, Pennsylvania. They felt that their role was to support what was happening at the center. They were also able to focus the congregation on providing those things that the government or the immediate community was not providing. Particularly important was the care for special needs children. They also felt it was important to conduct weekly chapel for the children. Again, it was not to make the children Lutheran but to provide the church as a frame of reference for them. These pastors felt that the church provided a safe place for the children to be educated.

Pastor Musser in Fox Chapel, Pennsylvania, appears to have more administrative oversight in the operation of the early childhood center of the congregation. While he is intentionally present at programs for the children and introduces himself, he also became very familiar with the day-care laws and regulations. In addition, he is an advocate for good teacher salaries and benefits. Each fall, the day-care staff and the Sunday school staff are installed during the Sunday liturgy. For him, it is important for the congregation to know that they have this important educational ministry.

Communication, partnership, shared ministry, being integrally involved: these are the descriptors of a healthy relationship among the pastor, congregation, and school. Melvin Kieschnick in *The Pastor and the Lutheran School* identifies eight descriptors that can model the pastor's role in a school:

- Shepherd—The pastor uses Law and Gospel to guide the flock to what the Holy Spirit has called them. The pastors who are called to congregations with schools or childhood centers have unusual opportunities to carry out this function.
- Theologian—The pastor is the principal theologian of the Lutheran congregation school. As such, she or he helps the school staff distinguish between Law and Gospel and helps teachers understand that the power for changed lives comes from the Gospel.
- Servant—The pastor is part of shared wisdom, which takes seriously the shared responsibility of the educational ministry. The pastor listens carefully to the contributions of staff, parents, and children.
- Leader—The pastor has a vision that is shared with others and comes out of an ethical context congruent with the call to be faithful to the Bible.
- Presence—The pastor is readily visible around the school. She or he is available for counsel, special school activities, etc.
- Advocate—The pastor is supportive of the school and early childhood ministry within the congregation as well as in the community. The pastor is also a spokesperson for children.
- Officiant—The pastor models reverence along with fidelity to the Gospel and respect for the Lutheran worship heritage.
- Peacemaker—The pastor may often be called upon to be an agent of peace in conflicts between people or groups of people. The pastor seeks to remind all that "God's seeking love reaches out to every member of the school family offering the peace of forgiveness with God."[8]

In a world in which our young people and their parents are often exposed to the difficulties and the turmoil of living with wars, violence, abuse, and so on, it is sometimes difficult to feel that we have a handle on living. Incidents like the school shootings at Columbine continue to occur. As we remember in the fall of each year the events of 9/11, we know that our lives as travelers were forever changed by those events. We can't get over it and, as I am from New York, I still can't go by the site. There is still anger and hurt by those events. In a roundtable discussion televised during the 9/11 commemorations, one grandmother talked about the drawings her preschool and kindergarten grandchildren were making. The drawings were not of dogs and cats, cars and bicycles, trees and flowers; they drew pictures of buildings being torn down and airplanes going into them. These are our young today. This is what they are envisioning as everyday life.

In a recent survey by Gallup, interviewees were asked an open-ended question about the most important issues for them. The top four issues were the situation in Iraq, terrorism, the economy, and immigration.[9] In regards to race relations, respondents were asked about the future of black/white relations in the United States. The majority of respondents from both races indicated that it would always be a problem (54 percent of whites and 58 percent of blacks).[10]

A report from the Barna Group is instructive for us as we examine Lutheran schools. While there are good feelings expressed about God by North Americans, living for God is not as important. There is a Sunday/Monday split. The Sunday experience is not lived out in the everyday working world of adults. Many feel that they are not in control of their lives.[11] This underscores the need for the church's educational ministries to continue to center on the teaching of God's continuing activity in human life. We humans are not at the center.

It is in this context—the world and the times in which we live—that we need to hear a different voice and a different word. It is within this context that our early childhood centers and day schools can assist in the growth and nurture of our young people in the Christian faith. By studying, learning, and worshipping, these young people will know that they are loved and cared for as children of God. They might grow up not to live in fear of the other, but to love the other, the stranger, the neighbor. They might grow up to tear down the walls that divide white, black, yellow, and brown citizens. This is not to say that this doesn't happen in other educational venues; it is to say that such love of those different from oneself is deliberate in these Lutheran communities of learning. The gospel has to be the center of all that is done.

Prior to teaching in higher education, Dr. Jeanie Payne, a professor of microbiology at Bergen Community College in New Jersey, taught at a Lutheran elementary school and high school for seven years while pursuing graduate studies. She recalls one student enrolled in the school who wanted to be a nurse. While the student's enthusiasm was great, she suffered from a learning disability that placed limitations on what she might be able to do in the health field. Teachers and counselors were able to identify her other gifts for helping those in need. With individualized care and concern by the staff searching vocational possibilities for her, she was able to complete high school and take a specialized course as a health aide that did not require the use of the cognitive thinking skills, which she otherwise would not have been able to achieve. Years later, she continues to work in the health-care field as well as be a wife and a mother. She was not left to fend for herself. She was cared for and loved at that Lutheran high school and continues to live a life of discipleship and to be involved in the church.

Evangelization, the active telling of the good news of Jesus Christ, can and does take place through our Lutheran schools. The goal of evangelization is not to reach out and make Lutherans of these students, but to excite and nurture disciples of Jesus rooted in the gospel using a Lutheran lens as a way of seeing God in the world. In these times of storm and stress for all, from young children to older adults, childhood centers and schools can assist young people and their parents in centering their lives on the gospel in order to live in this world. John Westerhoff, a religious educator, states that a radical understanding of parochial schools may be needed.[12] We are called to support and nurture those congregations and individuals called to this area of the church's ministry of education and evangelization.

Questions for Reflection and Conversation

1. How have you or those responsible for education and evangelization in your congregation helped new members become part of community life? How have new members, in turn, helped the congregation grow and learn?

2. How are interested visitors invited to become members of the congregation? Because each person is unique, what range of approaches might you use?

3. If your church has an early childhood center and/or school in what ways do you feel it reflects the Lutheran theological tradition?

4. What do you think is the theological focus of your early childhood center or school? What might it be if you had a center or school?

5. What qualities would you expect to see in a teacher in a Lutheran early childhood center of school? What is the pastor's role in the early childhood center of school of a congregation?

6. Examine Kieschnick's descriptors for the pastor and the Lutheran school? What might you add?

Parish Strategies

1. Talk with pastors, administrators, and teachers of Lutheran early childhood centers and/or schools in your area about the role of the center or school in the ministry of the congregation.

2. In order for your congregation to consider beginning an early childhood center or elementary school, contact the Director of Schools and Early Childhood Centers of the Evangelical Lutheran Church in America (1-800-NET-ELCA) and visit the Web site www.elca.org/schools. For an overview of resources, curricula, and accreditation processes, consult with the Evangelical Lutheran Education Association (www.eleanational.org).

> *Lutheran schools can be a pivotal place for evangelization of the young as well as their families.*

8. ABIDING IN THE WORD FOR THE SAKE OF THE WORLD

For all of us as Christians, our foundational identity comes from being "saved by grace through faith in Jesus Christ." Our salvation is sheer gift of God to us and not anything we have achieved on our own. But Lutheran pastor and author Kelly Fryer writes that we:

> have taken the gift for granted. And, in the meantime, there
> is a world that lies just outside our door, groaning in pain,
> hungry for anything that will fill it up and make it whole,
> wrecked by sin and longing to become everything it was
> created to be. . . . Somewhere along the way, we lost track of
> what the gift we have been given really is . . . Christ himself.
> And Christ comes with a call. *Christ comes with a call!*[1]

What do we do with this "world that lies just outside our door" and with this gift of grace which is really a call?

To begin with, we could take seriously eighteenth-century Methodist theologian, evangelist, and hymn writer John Wesley's example to make the world our parish, not our parish the world.[2] We can acquaint our congregations with the problems and pain, the hungers and longings, the wreckage and inequities of a world that is only a distorted shadow of what it was meant to be. This means offering Sunday morning forums and support groups for people living with disabilities, depression, or chronic illness. It means providing classes and guidance to members of the parish and members of the community trying to find their way through the maze of the health care system or prescription drug plans for seniors. It means offering presentations on bullying in schools, surviving divorce, parenting teenagers, and dealing with death. It means presenting sessions on the just-war theory, a series on peace in the Holy Land, or a panel discussion with Muslim, Palestinian, Christian, and Jewish panelists. Religious educational offerings like these are the least we can do to make the world our parish.

But there is, of course, more we could do with this "world that lies just outside our door" and with this gift of grace which is really a call. Jesus in the Gospel of John gave his disciples some unambiguous direction about what to do with this world waiting at the doorstep, which is really a gift and a call. To his disciples of every age, Jesus says, "abide, dwell, in my word." Jesus, in the fifteenth chapter of John's Gospel, uses the image of the vine and the branches, to say that the church grows by abiding in him, as he also abides in us (John 14:23; 15:3-5). "Abiding in Jesus" could be one overarching description of lifelong educational ministry. How do we abide in Jesus? By praying, by being immersed in his word, spoken and sung, by being fed and nourished on his body and blood. Only then can we produce the fruits of love.

Jesus sends us out into the world as he himself was sent into the world by the Father—out of love (John 20:19-21). Jesus adds that we should be in but not of the world (John 17:14-18). That means that we as the church are placed by Jesus with one foot squarely in the Word, which is Christ himself, and the other in the world, awkward and uncomfortable as that may be. This is the intersection, the crossroads, between Christian education and evangelism.

In this chapter we will look at two New Testament texts to discover what they might tell us about how to do evangelism with those whom God has placed at our doorstep. The two texts are: 1) the story of the first Pentecost (Acts 2:1-11); and 2) the story of Philip and the Ethiopian eunuch (Acts 8:26-39).

The Pentecost Story (Acts 2:1-11)

We have heard the story of the first Pentecost so often that it can seem to no longer hold any surprises for us. We know about the sound that came from heaven "like the rush of a violent wind" and the "tongues, as of fire" that rested on each of the apostles. We have heard how the disciples "were filled with the Holy Spirit and began to speak in other languages, as the Spirit gave them ability." We understand the basic implication of this text for today, of doing proclamation and Christian education in the native tongues of those ethnic groups whom we hope to reach—not like those first missionaries to the Chippewa Indians in and around the thumb of Michigan in the 1800s, who tried to turn the nomadic Native Americans into farmers and to teach them German in order to evangelize them.

A further implication of this text is sharing Christ "in the languages of people's daily lives," that is, in terms of their "vocation, relationships, location, and outlook"—especially their vocation.[3] Gender is a factor, too.

There has been much research in recent years about the differences between women's and men's reality in, for example, books like John Gray's *Men Are from Mars, Women Are from Venus.* Are there ways to do Christian education as evangelism so that women and men can hear the story of God's grace in Jesus Christ "each, in their own language"? And, conversely, are there ways in which we teach, methods or words that we use in our proclamation, that prevent women or men from hearing the message as good news for them?

Women Hearing in Their Own Language

In my various women's bible study groups are all kinds of women: historians, freelance writers, graphic designers, stay-at-home moms, nurses, local schoo-board members, lawyers, dieticians, teachers, and more. As Harvard psychologist Carol Gilligan pointed out in her groundbreaking book *A Different Voice*, relationships and interdependence are of primary importance for women, whether they were women in corporate America, in academia, or full-time mothers and homemakers.[4] So relationships and building community are important ingredients in any women's Bible study.

For several years, I have taught a weekly Bible study for moms from our church. They have felt free to invite their friends and neighbors, some of whom are churchgoers, some not. We have read and discussed books like Stephanie Paulsell's *Honoring the Body* and Joan Chittister's *The Story of Ruth: Twelve Moments in Every Woman's Life*. But most of the time, the women wanted to study the Bible itself. It takes us a while to work our way through a book of the Bible—some weeks we cover only a few verses, because they spurn questions and spirited discussion. But we have worked our way through Exodus, wandering through the wilderness with the children of Israel, not exactly for forty years, but close! We spent two years on the Gospel of John and are just concluding our second year studying Romans.

During our final session before summer break each year, I always ask the group what they will take with them into the summer. Last year, one of the members described sitting at home with her young daughter on her lap and looking out the window at a robin's nest in the rain gutter of the house next door. "This is what I feel like in this group," she said, "the warmth of a nest and being fed by the Word like the mother robin is feeding her children." After our study of John's Gospel one woman took with her that she had begun to see Jesus as "the Way, the Truth and the Life" (John 14:6). She had grown steadily in the faith and in her own self-confidence. She was eventually able to acknowledge to herself, and later, to the group, that she was a victim of domestic violence. She sought help and has now returned to school to prepare herself to resume a career outside the home.

Others in the group received emotional and spiritual support during a recurrence of depression, during the diagnosis of breast cancer and recovery from a mastectomy, and during parents' illnesses. There has been practical support offered during crises: meals delivered; children picked up and delivered back home from school, play practice, or sports. When a group member's husband—a former newspaper columnist—entered a nursing home because of early-onset Alzheimer's, she confessed how much she hated to visit her husband by herself. Members of the group offered to go with her. When another woman spoke of the difficulty she had in forgiving someone who had sued her doctor husband, other members of the group said, "Let us forgive him on your behalf until you are able to pray again and do so." Another group member spoke of how long it has taken her to forgive her father who had deserted her mother and eight children in Brazil years and years before, leaving them hungry and nearly penniless. This *is* hearing the gospel—and living in it! Group members now also feel more comfortable speaking their faith to friends and neighbors in a way that is inviting.

I was afraid, when we began our study of Romans that it would not have the richness of our study of Exodus or the Gospel of John, because Paul's focus in Romans is more on doctrine than narrative. I need not have worried. The participants in the group provided their own stories from real life to richly and poignantly illuminate the text. One day, we had a long discussion about the potential dangers facing their children on Internet Web sites. On another day, we gave thanks that the Spirit "intercedes for us with sighs too deep for words" (Romans 8:26-27). We confessed our faith that nothing—not worry, not illness, not the pace of our lives, not one's father going to jail for a crime he didn't commit, nothing—is able "to separate us from the love of God in Christ Jesus our Lord" (Romans 8:31-39).

We end each session with prayer for the needs of members and their families and friends. The Bible study group is an example of the church in miniature: one foot planted in and sustained by Jesus the Living Word—and by one another—and the other foot in the world, caring for families and friends, facing together whatever life throws at them. The group is also something of a safe house, a halfway house for members' neighbors and friends, who might not be ready to worship on a Sunday morning but are attracted to this welcoming, supportive community. This educational experience is also an evangelizing experience.

Men Hearing in Their Own Language

Men may need to connect their lives in the world with the Word in different ways than women. James Dittes, in his books *Men at Work* and *Driven by Hope: Men and Meaning*, writes about men talking about their relationship to their work; their disappointments; and their soft, unexpressed longings in the midst of being driven, disgruntled, even self-absorbed.[5]

Author David Murrow, in his book *Why Men Hate Going to Church*, contends that there are things that keep men away from church. He believes these practices are more conducive to the "feminine spirit" than to the masculine. Murrow often stereotypes the church, its teaching and practices, and exaggerates its failings; however, it is true that in 1998, over half of Baptist churches, 65 percent of Lutheran congregations, 70 percent of Methodist and Presbyterian churches, and 80 percent of Episcopal congregations had a gender gap of "at least 12 percent more women than men."[6] Most congregations also can easily identify a host of active, younger women in their parishes whose husbands seldom, if ever, enter the doors of a church.

While women might find comfort and support in Bible study, men are more attracted to challenges.[7] While in Bible study, women form relationships face-to-face and appreciate sitting in a circle. Men form relationships "side-by-side . . . while doing something else . . . painting a wall or working on a car."[8] Murrow suggests that churches need to "offer more project-based ministry opportunities"—local or overseas mission trips, habitat projects, or a service day to fix up homes or churches in the inner city. "Projects have a clear objective and an exit point," Murrow points out. "They're exciting to men."[9] My congregation's involvement in Hurricane Katrina relief and rebuilding projects are an example. The first mission trip—to the Gulf Coast of Mississippi—attracted several male college students who otherwise were not normally in church, along with thirty other men and women of all ages. All participated in the daily evening devotions and reflections on the people they met and helped during the day. A second trip—to "muck out" hurricane-flooded houses in New Orleans—included several father-and-son teams. Ages ranged from a fourteen-year-old high-school boy to young adults in their 20s and 30s to singles and couples in their 60s and 70s. There are seldom better opportunities in the church for intergenerational ministry than on mission trips like these. A third church team worked in Mississippi the next summer, and a fourth later returned to New Orleans. One young man who had been on the first three trips (one, working alongside his father) was co-leader of this last trip. He is "hooked" by this kind of church volunteer service.

Another church member, whose wife and two daughters are in church every Sunday, but who seldom came with them, went on the first mission trip and prepared an excellent video-slide report for presentation at Sunday services. Men like to learn "through personal discovery" and "hands-on experience" rather than have answers provided for them.[10]

Most men, regardless of their church involvement, find time spent out in nature and in sports "profoundly significant in nurturing and expressing their identity and spirituality."[11] Playing team sports or hiking in the mountains or by a lakeshore is more than just recreation for men. It is part of their identity and creates a bonding experience.[12] It is important to engage young men theologically: connecting them to the struggles of the incarnate Christ, who wrestled with his true identity in the wilderness. Regarding the Luke 4:1-13 account of Jesus's temptation in the wildernessand the authors wrote:

> Here we find God incarnate wandering in nature, amidst the mountains, valleys, deserts, and rocks. [Jesus] is physically challenged and pushed to his limits lacking food and water. Power, material wealth, and false worship are laid out before him. At this moment, Jesus confronts issues that many young men are facing. . . . This Jesus of the wilderness could strike a familiar chord with the young male spiritual quest.[13]

Many young men, churchgoers as well as those with no church affiliation, think of Jesus only as a moral role model; they have little or no "awareness of the substance and power of Jesus" for their lives.[14] Christian education as evangelism for men must include much more than providing outdoor activities or utilizing the language or metaphor of sports. It needs to include Bible study and worship in the outdoor setting that proclaims the meaning and purpose of Jesus's life and its connection with our lives. Jesus was tempted, as we are tempted, by power and the aggrandizement of goodies and the false gods who promise us everything and deliver little. Jesus, through the cross, forgives us when we succumb to life's temptations and calls us through his resurrection to begin a new life in him.

Men want and need to hear the good news of Jesus in their own language. What specifically might that mean in our teaching? Murrow says the church's language about being lost and saved doesn't work for men, because men "hate to be lost; that's why they don't ask for directions." A more helpful term for men is the one Jesus used more frequently in the Gospels to call disciples: "follow me," which appeals to men because it is action-oriented, not passive.[15] "Christianity based on risk avoidance will never attract men," Murrow contends.[16] The story of the temptation of Jesus speaks to men of what is worth "high risk" behavior and what is not. Jumping off the temple to prove his identity as the Son of God and to prove God's protection of him (Luke 4:9-13) were not what Jesus came into the world to do. It was in being broken to heal a broken world and commending his Spirit to God, even as he drew his last breath on the cross (Luke 23:44-46) that Jesus risked all he had and all he was for us—men and women.

Murrow says men are asking, is the church really the "power of God unleashed on earth, or is it just religious activity? . . . A religious life will not capture a man's imagination; only an unpredictable adventure with Christ will do."[17] Will we, in our teaching and reaching out to the world at our doorstep, offer that adventure to men and women too?

In the above two sections of this chapter, I am not trying to pigeonhole, or stereotype, either men or women. Saint Paul wrote that, "in Christ," there is "no longer Jew or Greek, there is no longer slave or free, there is no longer male and female," for all are "one in Christ Jesus" (Gal. 3:28). In the sixteenth chapter of Romans, Paul lists twenty-five names, including Jewish names, Roman names, and Greek names. There are slave names and free people's names. There are men's names and women's names. This list is instructive for the church, today and in every age. It does not give evidence of the church as patriarchal (as it was for so many centuries), or of the feminization of the church (as some accuse the church of doing today).

Paul mentions Phoebe, a deacon, or minister, of the church at Cenchreae, who "has been a benefactor of many and of myself as well." The Greek word *prostatis* literally means "one who stands before." It can also carry the meaning of "president" or "leader." Paul also sends greetings to Prisca and Aquila, wife and husband (the wife is mentioned first as the more prominent one). The couple served as theology tutors to Apollus in Ephesus (see Acts 18:24-25). Paul adds greetings to Mary, "who has worked very hard among you"; to Andronicus and Junia (probably husband and wife) who, Paul says, "are prominent among the apostles" and were "in Christ" before Paul was. (Rom.16:1-16)

We want a church today where men and women are full partners in ministry, in leading and serving, in learning and evangelizing, so that it might grow in Christ.

Philip and the Ethiopian Eunuch (Acts 8:26-39)

How does the church grow?

Church-growth experts today would have us believe that there are several ingredients needed for a congregation to experience big growth: to be located in a homogeneous community; to have room for a stadium-sized parking lot; to have a large overhead screen in the sanctuary to project an outline of the pastor's sermon and the words to the hymns, plus a praise band to lead the congregational singing.

Nowhere in Scripture are any of the above elements mentioned.

So how *does* the church grow?

The love displayed by early Christians for one another—rich and poor, slave and free, Jew and Gentile—was the single most important factor in the extraordinary growth of the church in the first century. "Behold, how they love one another," the rest of the society exclaimed. Loving and sacrificing and caring for one another is still a compelling witness for individuals looking for a church to belong to today.

But how does the church grow?

According to Acts, the church grows by the Spirit's leading and guiding. An angel of the Lord told Philip to head out on the wilderness road that went down from Jerusalem to Gaza, to head for what we know today as the Gaza Strip (Acts 8:26-39). On this wilderness road there was a chariot carrying home a court official of the queen of Ethiopia, a eunuch who was in charge of the royal treasury and who had probably been castrated as a condition for his post. He was a God-fearer, a Gentile who was returning home from worshiping the God of Israel in Jerusalem. Seated in his chariot, he was reading the prophet Isaiah. The Spirit directed Philip to "go over to the chariot, and join it." So Philip ran up to the chariot.

The movie *Chariots of Fire* told the story of two British runners, one Jewish, Harold Abrahams, and the other a devout Christian, Eric Liddell, both of whom won gold medals in the 1924 Olympics. The "chariots of fire" of the title were the runners themselves, burning up the paths and the tracks they ran on, with the sheer joy of running. At the direction of the Spirit, Liddell left competitive running in 1925 to become a missionary in China. He served there for twenty years before he died in a Japanese internment camp a few months before the end of World War II.

So how does the church do evangelism? It begins as Philip shows us, and Eric Liddell also, by running along side of others, listening to their questions and accompanying them, when invited, in their struggles—as the Ethiopian eunuch "invited Philip to get in and sit beside him" and guide him (Acts 8:29-31). More often than not, people are trying to understand more than a Scripture passage. They are trying to "read" what is happening in their own lives, too.

The Ethiopian wanted to know who this "suffering servant" was whom Isaiah was describing in Isaiah 53 (Acts 8:32-35) and how his suffering connected to the Ethiopian's own situation. Then and now, people are seeking to discover what Jesus's giving up his life has to do with the inconsistencies and paradoxes with which we live, with our unfixable pasts and uncertain futures. How does Jesus's suffering and death intersect with our joys and reframe our sorrows, those events in our past which we regret with all our heart?

Something happened when Philip hopped onboard that chariot on the Gaza wilderness road. The Ethiopian heard that Jesus's death was not the end of the story but that Jesus chose to be wounded to make others whole.

When the Ethiopian eunuch had worshipped in Jerusalem, he would not have been allowed into the temple proper because he was a foreigner and castrated ("not whole"). But his chariot-of-fire conversion would doubly fulfill the prophecy of Isaiah 56: no more "let the foreigner . . . say, 'The Lord will surely separate me from his people'"; no more "let the eunuch say, 'I am just a dry tree'" (Isaiah 56:3). For God pledges: "To the eunuchs who . . . choose the things that please me . . . I will give . . . a name better than sons and daughters; I will give them an everlasting name that shall not be cut off" (vv. 4-5). It is no wonder that, when they came to some water along the way, the Ethiopian asked, "What is to prevent me from being baptized?" Then and there in the water, he received his everlasting name. The eunuch was no longer a dry tree; in baptism, he became a green branch bearing much fruit. According to Christian tradition, that is exactly what the eunuch did: "bear fruit," carrying the gospel of new life in Christ back to his own country and people. And so do we.

Hearing and Responding to People's Questions Today

We began this chapter with the Kelly Fryer quote about the "world that lies just outside our door, groaning in pain, hungry for anything that will fill it up and make it whole, wrecked by sin and longing to become everything it was created to be." These people outside our door, not connected with any church, some having drifted away from prior membership, often have questions, spoken or unspoken, that block belief. Many of these questions deal with their own suffering and with their conceptions or misconceptions about God. What they are seeking is someone like Philip, who is willing to accompany them, run or walk alongside them in their struggle and doubt. This means that the first call of members of the church is to accompany neighbors, friends, and work colleagues in their journey through life and, when invited, to be mentors to them.

The church often makes the mistake of creating curriculum for seekers and potential new members that begins with the answers the church has, rather than with the questions seekers bring. Inquirers might be more ready to receive what the church has to offer in Christ Jesus if we begin like Philip did on the desert road with the Ethiopian eunuch—with the questions individuals have about faith and life. There are new member materials designed to begin with inquirers' questions, to address where seekers "are on their spiritual journey."[18] Evangelizing congregations also can create their own education series to respond to the doubts and questions nonchurchgoers have. Theologian Paul Tillich once said, "Doubt is not the opposite of faith; it is one element of faith." Maybe Christian education as evangelism, therefore, needs to begin with people's doubts.

A congregation could offer classes called For Doubters Only or Life's Unanswerable Questions or create a Bible study for doubting Thomases, as one Lutheran parish in rural Iowa does. The class could be publicized in local community papers with invitations also sent to inactive church members. Perhaps the class would be designed especially for the nonchurchgoing husbands or wives of those active in the church or for parents of baptized children who drop off their kids for Sunday school but don't regularly attend church.

A class could begin in an open-ended mode, with attendees responding to: "Things I've Never Understood about Life," or "Gripes I've Always Had about God, but Was Afraid to Say Out Loud," with subsequent sessions addressing the issues and gripes that have emerged. One possible question to begin with might be the one the disciples asked Jesus when he was asleep at the rudder in the back of the boat in the midst of a violent storm on the Sea of Galilee: "Master, do you not care that we are perishing?" (Mark 4:38) Perhaps that kind of question would lead to a discussion of what attendees think God is like and how much they think God is engaged in the world, how much, that is, they think God (Jesus) cares about them and this world.

Speaking to People's Concept of God

In a survey of religious beliefs conducted by the Gallup Poll on behalf of Baylor University's Institute for Studies of Religions, respondents "offered 16 words to characterize God, such as *motherly*, *wrathful*, and *severe*. It supplied 10 descriptions related to God's involvement in the world, including 'a cosmic force in the universe,' 'removed from world affairs,' and 'concerned with my personal well-being.'" These questions "turned up four ways in which people conceive of deity,"[19] or basically four different "Gods," based on "how engaged people think God is in the world and how angry God is with the world."[20]

The four basic types of "Gods" are:

- an authoritarian God who is very judgmental, metes out punishment, and is highly involved in world and personal affairs
- a benevolent God who is also active in the world and individual lives, but more forgiving
- a critical God who is not engaged, but still passes judgment
- a distant God who sets the laws of nature in motion but is completely removed from worldly affairs

The kind of "God" a person has, their view of God's character or personality type, has some major implications for religious education and outreach. For example, "36 percent of those unaffiliated with any specific religion believe in the Distant God."

Women tend more toward thinking of a Benevolent God, while men are more likely to think of God as angry. "Thinking God is angry, however," one researcher reported, "does not necessarily lead people to a place of worship." Rather, the researchers found, "people are sitting in the pews because they feel personally engaged with God or that God is personally engaged in their lives."[21]

Anne Neufeld Rupp, in her book for parents and church teachers, *Growing Together: Understanding and Nurturing Your Child's Faith Journey,* points out that "our life and relationships may be influenced by beliefs about God of which we are not even aware. Some beliefs may dominate our lives; others may creep in during times of crisis."[22] These beliefs about God that parents are largely unaware of affect not only their faith, but their children's faith as well. If we view God as the Creator who has "then left us to fend for ourselves,"[23] or if a sense of being forsaken in a crisis "becomes an inner belief that God is always remote and distant," that belief of ours may influence our children more than what they learn about God in Sunday school. "We constantly feel guilty and live in fear of being punished" because we view God as "a judge who watches and angrily lets us know how bad we are," that mindset may communicate itself more clearly to our youngsters than the church's teaching that God is love. If our inner belief is that "it is God's job to make us happy and to make us feel good," [24] what does this view communicate to our child about God when illness, death, or job loss strikes the family? Discovering and exploring individuals' images of God is an integral part of the ministry of education and evangelism.

Some Words to Go and Grow On

In Luke's Gospel, when Jesus called Simon Peter from the lakeshore to be his disciple, Jesus said, "Don't be afraid; from now on you will be catching people" (Luke 5:1-11). The word for catching people in the original Greek meant to "take them alive." The ideas presented in this chapter, therefore, are not designed to dangle some bait before people's eyes, get them to swallow it "hook, line and sinker," and then "drag" them, flailing and fighting and gasping for air, into the church's net.

Just the opposite. The ideas presented are intended to help us, first of all, not to be afraid to engage those who are on our doorstep . . . and beyond. The gift of grace we have been given in the Gospel is Christ himself, and Christ comes with a call!

And secondly, the ideas to help men and women hear the good news, each in their own language, and the suggestions for how the church can accompany those who have questions as they travel on a desert road are all ways in which to "take people alive," so that they might experience the fullness of life that God offers in Christ Jesus.

To change the metaphor of a world lying at our door, there are people around us who are living their lives in "shallow water," knowing that there must be more to life than what they experience day after day. There are people around us who have messed up their lives, who are treading furiously in deep water, and are barely managing to keep from going under.

Like Peter and the other disciples, known and unknown, down through the ages, Jesus is calling us to catch these people alive in the nets of God's love and to help them discover for themselves the fullness and joy of the life Jesus came to give a whole world in need.

Questions for Reflection and Conversation

1. How does your congregation share good news so that both men and women can hear it in their own language?

2. When and where did you begin to understand that the gift of grace we have been given is Christ himself, and that Christ comes with a call?

3. Are there Bible stories or texts that have profoundly shaped you in your discipleship and mission in the world? What are they and how have they formed you?

4. Are there opportunities in your ministry of Christian education for people to ask the questions they are wrestling with or to talk about their views of God?

Parish Strategies

1. Do an analysis of your congregational membership. Is there a gender gap between men and women? Who are the young men in your parish community, beyond the doors of the church? Identify the nonchurchgoing husbands of active women members.

2. Appoint a men's task force that includes, younger, older, active, and inactive men. Plan one or two pilot events (a wilderness trip, a service project, a mission trip, etc.) to reach out to men with opportunities to work and talk about faith "side by side."

3. Analyze the number and types of educational opportunities and mission trips or service projects your congregation offers each year. Consider adding additional ones. Make sure there is a component of Bible study or worship in every service event and some service component as part of every parish Bible study.

4. Develop a Christian education series for doubters or those with questions about God, suffering or other life issues. Publicize the class in community newspapers and on your Web site and send invitations to church inactives.

> *"Abide, Dwell in My Word" could be an overarching description of lifelong educational ministry.*

PART THREE

CLAIMING THE CHALLENGE

9. GO AND MAKE LEARNERS! SUPPORTING TRANSFORMATION IN EDUCATION AND EVANGELISM

Mary E. Hess

"Go, therefore, and make disciples of all nations, baptizing them in the name of the Father, and of the Son, and of the holy Spirit, teaching them to observe all that I have commanded you"
—Matthew 28:19

This phrase has reverberated throughout Christian communities of faith over the centuries, particularly those that have found their identity in the sharing of the gospel. But what does it really mean to "make disciples?" One of the root meanings of the Greek word μαθητευω is that of "apprentice," or "learner." It might be far more useful in our current contexts to translate this phrase as "go and make learners." Yet in many ways, "making learners" is the opposite of much that has been done in the name of discipling and mission. Far too often, the impulse to share the good news has been combined with a very narrow definition of teaching and learning. This definition and experience of learning has led to enormous pain and oppression, as Christians have sought to impose their beliefs on others. Yet how might we help each other—and members of our communities of faith—transform our understandings of teaching and learning?

Robert Kegan, an adult learning theorist, has teamed up with Lisa Lahey in an extensive exploration of change. They have proposed some concrete ways to support transformation among adults that is both constructive and lasting. At the heart of their process is a series of "revisions" or "reframings" of common ways in which we talk. Their book—*How the Way We Talk Can Change the Way We Work*—describes these reframings in terms of seven languages, seven ways of describing the world and ways of working with it that invite us into habits, into practices that shape and support transformation.[1] Kegan and Lahey describe four personal, or internal, languages and three social languages. Woven together, these seven languages draw people toward patterns of practice that make the community of truth a very present reality. While their book is not explicitly theological, their ideas extend very easily and constructively into pastoral contexts and provide rich nourishment for evangelism oriented as learning.

From Complaint to Commitment

The first language is one that they describe as, "moving from complaint to commitment." Kegan and Lahey's assertion is that, deep within our complaints lie corresponding commitments that give rise to the complaint. Seeking to understand the commitment brings a different and more constructive energy to the situation. When Lutheran congregation members complain about door knocking as a strategy of evangelism, is it the strategy itself they are critiquing? Is there an underlying commitment to open inquiry that they seek to preserve? In other words, if their personal experience of door-knock evangelism is limited to Jehovah's Witnesses or salespeople intent on selling the newest product, they might equate such a practice with close-minded repetition of a specific position, rather than open inquiry.

In contexts in which we are trying to help church members move outside of their usual boxes and find out who is in the neighborhood, it might be more appropriate to think about the practice of door knocking as one of inquiry: Who lives in the neighborhood? What are their concerns and needs? How might our church respond?

The language of complaint is found in our own learning as teachers as well. Many of the complaints I find myself voicing—or perhaps venting would be a better word when I am tired!—have at their heart a deeper commitment. Forcing myself to state an issue as a positive commitment, rather than as a negative whine, both affirms such a commitment and frames it in a way that empowers me.[2] When I complain that adults in my church never have time to volunteer with children, I am really pointing to my deeper sense that the children in our parish need time with adults outside of their own families. But *have* I provided ways for adults to perceive their own journeys of faith as important stories to share with younger members of our church? *Especially* the stories of their own doubts and dilemmas? Looked at it in this way, I am forced to acknowledge that my complaint holds the seeds of its own resolution. This language leads naturally to Kegan and Lahey's second language: that of moving from a language of blame to one of personal responsibility.

From Blame to Personal Responsibility

One way in which Kegan and Lahey speak of this language is to ask the question: "What are you doing, or not doing, that is keeping your commitment from being more fully realized?" Right now in the Lutheran church, there is a significant amount of writing and other energy directed at pointing to the ways in which the ELCA appears to be evangelical in name only: "Lutherans don't want to share their faith"; "Lutherans don't have a missional bone in their body"; "to be evangelical one cannot be Lutheran," and so on.[3]

At first, my underlying assumption is that mission—sharing the gospel with others—is at the heart of learning, and hence crucial to engagement in contemporary ministry. But when I ask myself what I am doing, or not doing, that keeps this commitment from being realized, I begin to consider my complaint from a different angle. Why don't my fellow congregational members want to share their faith? What about the process has taught them that it is not appropriate? In asking these questions, I can begin to get at deeper elements of the dilemma. Perhaps they are not sure enough of what they believe to share it and fear letting on that they aren't certain. Perhaps they have had bad experiences with other people sharing faith and have felt their own faith diminished in the process. They certainly do not want to inflict that experience on someone else!

Perhaps I, as religious educator or as a pastoral leader in a particular context, have not helped further an understanding of the joy of sharing faith stories or helped the stories come alive for people. Given the cultural contexts we inhabit, a postmodern turn of mind rarely accepts assertions—particularly from institutional authorities—as a priori correct. Just because I have *told* people that Christian theology draws us outward in mission, that does not mean that they accept that assertion. How can I help them sympathetically identify with such an understanding? How can I engage them, provide enough routes into the idea and enough immediate connecting points, that they begin to see, in their own imagination, in their own experiences, how faith and mission might be connected? Do I even know how to go about inviting them effectively into the material I wish to share? And if I do not, does that mean I am unqualified for my current role as a pastoral leader? Such doubts emerge all too often in the work of teaching, and all too often, there are few places to voice, let alone explore, such questions.

Part of the dilemma I have found is that, it is not enough to work with these issues on the cognitive level; the affective and the psychomotor levels carry at least as much power in shaping student understanding. That is to say, we need to work not simply with assertions of *ideas,* but also seriously consider people's feelings and support their actions. So the very way I approach the concerns of adults in my congregation teaches them something about whether their concerns matter. This, in turn, teaches them something about their own faith. The same is true about my own doubts. Do I simply push them down and ignore them? Do I too often use that misdirected internal energy to blame the learners for their problems? Or do I ask myself the questions that bring me beyond individualism and break open room for the Spirit to enter in?

Recognizing that I bear some personal responsibility in the situation is not, of course, to assume that I carry all of it and that the people in our congregations bear none. As author Parker Palmer notes, teaching in the community of truth demands an engagement with the truth at the heart of the circle of knowing; it demands that there be a *there* around which we gather.[4] I bear responsibility. My fellow congregants bear responsibility. And together, we meet in a specific context and around a specific topic that carries its own substance and center.

From New Year's Resolutions to Competing Commitments

Recognizing the larger context in which we are embedded moves us to Kegan and Lahey's third language, that of moving from New Year's resolutions to competing commitments. Most of us are familiar with New Year's resolutions—those bright and cheery resolutions to begin the New Year afresh—to lose 10 pounds, to pray regularly, to invite one person to church, and so on. Kegan and Lahey point out that one of the problems with such resolutions is that they do not take into account the reality that many commitments coexist, and often conflict, with each other. The language of resolutions also tends to put a negative spin on the task at hand, given all of the times I am not successful in keeping them.

I may be committed to praying with my children every day, but I am also committed to making sure they are fed nutritious food, clothed in clean clothing, and have finished their homework before they go to bed. If I cannot manage ten minutes of family devotion every day, then surely it is a failure on my part. Yet in a world of twenty-four-hour days, there may not be time to do everything well. Facing the challenge of recognizing one's own limitations requires the ability to move outside of oneself to consider these competing commitments, as well as the specific underlying assumptions that may be preventing us from effectively meeting them.

I know that, far too often, I am tired and frustrated at the end of the day. Spending ten minutes of reflective time with my children seems like more than is possible, when all I want to do is get them into bed, so that I can finish my chores and go to sleep myself. Alternatively, getting up half an hour early so that we can share together seems daunting with the press of morning tasks. These very same pressures face most of the adults with children in our congregations. Prayer time becomes yet another chore, rather than a pause that can refresh. Evangelism—even with our own children!—seems like another demand, rather than a natural practice. But when we do find ways to build "faith talk" time into daily practice in ways that build refreshment and joy into the day, we shift the notion of religious education from one of instructional duty to one of shared practice.

The corresponding implicit curriculum—that evangelism and/or religious instruction must be done in a certain way—and beneath it, the unvoiced null curriculum[5] of, "it has always been done this way, and if we do not continue to do it this way the whole church will fall apart"—holds powerful sway. As Palmer writes, the "great things" at the heart of our engagement can demand more of us than we recognize and shape more of our teaching and learning than we are ready to admit that they do.[6] It is at this point that the final language of Kegan and Lahey's four personal languages—the foundation of their mental machinery model—becomes so important.

From Assumptions that Hold Us to Assumptions We Hold

Kegan and Lahey assert that we need to move from the language of big assumptions that hold us to the language of assumptions that we hold. This is a key element of transformational learning. What was once "subject"—what once held us to the point that we could not see it—becomes "object," or something that we can now hold out and consider. One of the biggest assumptions to pervade religious education is that of teaching authority, that of the difference between the objectivist myth of teaching and learning critiqued in Palmer's work and the more relational, connected model he supports.[7]

The objectivist, instrumental model of teaching assumes that the acknowledged authority best mediates interaction with the topic under consideration. Indeed, that model suggests that such interaction is essentially unidirectional, proceeding at the invitation of the teacher and in the direction the teacher outlines. How much more painful is such an assumption for evangelism! If only we, as the evangelizers, hold the truth to be shared, consider the dangerous consequences if we are wrong or if we fail. Indeed, it seems to me that some of the panicky energy that can be felt in discussions of mission and evangelism in the Lutheran Church grows out of this inadequate model. As long as we are held by this assumption, it is impossible to question it, even to begin to build a relationship to it, rather than being held by it. Perhaps it is true, but how can we know unless we consider other alternatives? How can we know, unless we can imagine our way into a space in which it is not the case?

I am convinced that part of the challenge I face in my own attempts to share faith with others comes from this unexamined assumption; so much flows outward from it, not the least being religious education programs that are modelled on typical classrooms with paper-and-pencil texts or confirmation curricula that are heavy on doctrine and light on faith practice. Perhaps the analogy to art education is apt. Most art educators will argue that children are natural artists, but they become schooled away from their creativity in classroom settings where they learn to "draw within the lines" and sculpt clay into recognizable figures. Religious educators who spend thoughtful and engaged time with young children will tell you that they are natural evangelists, asking deep questions of the world around them and attending to its intricacy and beauty in ways few adults can match. But these same children learn to let go of such questions and thin their attention to such a degree that, by the time they are in confirmation classes, their faith has shrunk down to a commitment to "jump through the hoop" so that their parents are happy, rather than a deepening of their attention and a related ability to raise key questions.

Perhaps we need to remember Paul's words to the Corinthians, "I did not come with sublimity of words or of wisdom. For I resolved to know nothing except Jesus Christ and him crucified" (1 Cor. 2: 1-5 NAB).

What does it mean to know nothing except Jesus Christ and him crucified? Surely not that we all should simply show up and wait passively for information to be showered upon us. But what kind of learning environment creates an active space of listening for such a revelation? What kind of design can structure the space to allow for the best opportunity for such engagement? What kind of learning is transformational? What kind of education is evangelism? This question is the fulcrum of Kegan and Lahey's work as well, for the four languages just described build a foundation for change; however, they need to be embedded in the social languages that Kegan and Lahey delineate.

From Prizes and Praising to Ongoing Regard

The first of these social languages is the movement from the language of prizes and praising to that of ongoing regard. One way to think about this shift is deeply theological: it is moving away from a space in which one's actions earn merit to one in which one is gifted simply by being a child of God. In other words, it is the difference between a world of earned merit and one of overflowing, unmerited, and unearned, but freely available *grace*.

Do members of our congregations understand themselves as fully capable evangelists, gifted with unique stories that must be shared to enable learning for everyone to come alive? Or do they instead enter our churches seeking to discover, in the shortest time possible, what the church wants and how to display it so that they can stay in relationship? Or even worse, do they enter our churches just seeking some quiet respite from the outside world, rather than deeper engagement in creation with God in the midst of it?

Are our practices of religious education—particularly within structured adult learning programs—focused on passing along certain information to passive students and thus equipping them? Or are they focused on recognizing and noting our experiences of God, both positive and challenging, leaving students *informed* (but not *deformed*) by our words? For example, "Martin, thank you for being such an attentive learner," versus, "Martin, I appreciate the way in which your questions caused me to think in new ways about what this text means." The first statement attributes a trait to the learner. The second describes how the learner had an impact on my own learning. It is the second form that encourages evangelical learning.

Kegan and Lahey note that this kind of language:

> Distributes precious information that one's actions have significance; infuses energy *into* the system; communicates appreciation or admiration directly to the person; communicates *specific* information to the person about the speaker's personal experience of appreciation or admiration; *non-attributive*, characterizes the speaker's experience, and not the person being appreciated; sincere and authentic, more halting and freshly made; transformational potential for both the speaker and the person being regarded . . . [9]

Providing a *variety* of ways in which adults can share their faith and, in doing so, learn more about the community of faith in which they find themselves, communicates something very different from offering only a single, foury-five minute class between liturgies. There are so many ways adults can be creatively involved. Providing opportunities for adults to take the risk of trying something they are *not* good at, with deliberate incentives for trying something new and difficult rather than steep penalties for failing, contributes to an environment of ongoing regard.[10] Sharing one's faith with a friend is hard enough, let alone with a stranger. But what about making a collage of magazine pictures that attempts to describe who God is? Or spending a day fishing, and then coming back to share three things one observed about God's Creation?

In the seminary context, I often use critical incident reports, described by Stephen Brookfield, to communicate to my students that their experience of the learning event matters.[11] How often do we provide real room for adult learners in a congregation to share their experience of learning? How often we do move outside of our own realms of expertise and join them in theirs? When was the last time that we visited congregation members in their workplaces and asked them to articulate what it means to be a person of faith in that context? To do so, I believe we need to make very clear, first, that we are not seeking a specific doctrinal voicing; rather, we are genuinely curious about what they are learning about God and about their relationship with Jesus Christ in a context in which such language is often forbidden. As Craig Van Gelder notes: "Interestingly, just as the church is reponsible to read and relate to its context in order to better translate the gospel and specific church forms, so also the context reads and changes the church in relation to its efforts to present the gospel."[12] How do we create room for the *context* in which we are embedded to contribute to our own learning, for the *context* to evangelize the church?

As these are clearly social languages that Kegan and Lahey are describing, their implementation must stretch beyond any individual congregation or church. Set within the often competing commitments of secular society, creating an environment of ongoing regard can be very difficult. Yet there are ways of doing so, not the least being using the core theological categories at the heart of our belief system as central organizing principles rather than defaulting to those of the wider culture. Rather than organizing religious education and evangelism in terms of prizes going to those whose programs draw the largest number of people, it is possible to organize religious education in terms of matching people's God-given gifts to specific tasks and roles. It is possible to think about a congregation nourishing people and supporting them in their vocations *in the world* as a primary means of evangelism. Perhaps we should be asking, "What is the impact of our congregation on this context?" and "Who would miss us if we were not here?" rather than "How many people are coming through our doors?"[13]

In my local parish, it is clear that certain people are gifted as pastoral leaders, others as advocates, still others as parents, as political leaders, as retail clerks, as cleaning people, or as teachers, and so on. The vocation of each is vital, and the process of sharing faith in each setting is unique. Providing room for each set of gifts to be identified and given room to flourish contributes to an overall atmosphere quite different from that in which congregational ministry usually exists. It also inevitably creates constructive synergy that spreads energy, as opposed to stress-filled busy-ness that simply saps energy. It embodies, very visibly, the community of truth Palmer describes and which, I believe, is at the heart of evangelical mission.

From Rules and Policies to Public Agreement

Deliberately moving in these directions, however, tends to be moving against the grain of much current pastoral ministry. It, therefore, requires the next language that Kegan and Lahey have identified: that which notes a difference between rules and policies as opposed to the language of public agreement. Most of us are quite familiar with what is meant by "rules and policies"—these are explicit statements in most organizations. Rules and policies are almost universally developed at the top of an organization and rarely provide constructive ground for engagement. You may know when you have broken a rule, for instance, but much like the language of prizes and praising, the language of rules and policies is observed more in the nature of its application to violations, rather than in proactive, ongoing ways.

The language of public agreement, by way of contrast, is a "vehicle for responsible people to collectively imagine a public life they simultaneously know they would prefer and know they will, at times, fall short of."[14] This is the language of covenant, rather than contract. It is a language of relationship, of commitment to each other, of repentance, and of forgiveness. It is a language that teachers often ask small groups to develop at the beginning of a collaborative process: What will be our agreement about collaboration? How will we know if we are indeed living into it? Such agreements allow individual members of a group space in which to call the group into accountability. It is a language that demands, as well as facilitates, participation. I would go so far as to argue that much of Paul's rhetoric in the letters to the scattered churches of the first century is an attempt to articulate such a language.

At the beginning of each adult learning event that I facilitate, we spend some time exploring this notion of a language of public agreement. One obvious example involves agreeing with those present that stories that are shared in this context stay here, unless someone explicitly gives permission to share them in other settings. All of my events are designed with room for improvisation; helping each other understand what that can mean begins in the first session of any such learning event.

From Constructive to Deconstructive Criticism

The final language that Kegan and Lahey describe is that which moves from the language of constructive criticism to that of deconstructive criticism. This relates to both education and evangelism. Given how most of us were trained to practice constructive criticism, it can be jarring to recognize the assumptions upon which it rests. For instance, constructive criticism:

> assumes the perspective of the feedback giver is right and correct. . . . An accompanying assumption is that there is only one right answer. . . . As long as we hold our view to be true—we have a vested interest in maintaining the truth. . . . Once we establish our meaning as the standard and norm against which we evaluate other people, we essentially hold them to our personal preferences.[15]

Criticizing constructive criticism is not an argument for the impossibility of normative truth. Rather, Kegan and Lahey point beyond notions of destructive and constructive criticism to what they have instead labeled "deconstructive criticism," a term that assumes that offering criticism is an opening for engagement in real dialogue that seeks to foster substantial learning. Such engagement rests on a series of "deconstructive propositions":

1. There is probable merit to my perspective.
2. My perspective may not be accurate.
3. There is some coherence, if not merit, to the other person's perspective.
4. There may be more than one legitimate interpretation.
5. The other person's view of my viewpoint is important information in assessing whether I am right or identifying what merit there is to my view.
6. Our conflict may be the result of the separate commitments each of us holds, including commitments we are not always aware we hold.
7. Both of us have something to learn from the conversation.
8. We need to have two-way conversations to learn from each other.
9. If contradictions can be a source of learning, then we can come to engage not only internal contradictions as a source of learning, but interpersonal contradictions (i.e., "conflict") as well.
10. The goal of our conversation is for each of us to learn more about ourself and the other as meaning makers.[16]

Note how these propositions shift us from the mode of being the owners of truth to being seekers of truth. Quite visibly, they move us from processes of indoctrination or proselytism to more relational and dynamic models for a community of learning. In making this move, we rely on our faith that there is, indeed, truth to be discovered—but our very faith shapes the humility of our search for truth.[17]

These propositions are bases by which to begin a true conversation. They are a clear foundation for the kind of learning involved in discipleship. As Paul notes, "I come not bearing wise words of wisdom, but only Christ, and him crucified." Paul knows something of what he speaks, having had his entire life turned upside down, quite literally struck from his stance into blindness and turned to a new road. It is important to recognize that:

> A language of deconstructive criticism is not a language of discounting one's own negative evaluation. Rather it's about holding two simultaneous realities together. And practicing a language for deconstructive conflict does not leave one in paralysis of analysis, unable to act, merely better understanding the conflict. Finally, language for deconstructive conflict is not practiced first of all for the purpose of making the conflict disappear or even reducing its intensity.[18]

Indeed, this kind of language can, at times, heighten awareness of the differences that exist in a given situation. Imagine what this kind of conversation makes possible among differing generations in a specific context, among differing denominations, or among differing faiths!

It is an argument *for* the nuanced and complex notion of truth that Palmer identifies as *troth,* or the truth for which one gives one's life.[19] Such truth is neither easily derived nor simply specified. This is the kind of truth for which Jesus was crucified and on the basis of which we as sinful human beings are redeemed. This is also the truth—through pledging of troth—that most often poses the really painful dilemmas of growth for our learners and ourselves.

Fundamentally, educators know that learning brings transformation. Fundamentally, evangelists know that sharing the good news brings transformation. What we have to remember is that transformation is at least as often *our own* as it is anyone or anything else's. When the Gospel pushes for a missional emphasis, these stories invite us into "troubling the waters." They invite us into the currents of a large and tumultuous river leading to an even larger ocean. They invite us ever more deeply into our own brokenness and, paradoxically, into the joy of God's gift of grace in spite of that brokenness.

We need, at once, to trust that our faith can carry us beyond that brokenness, and that our despair at our brokenness is but the starting point of our joy. This experience, this learning, is at the heart of evangelism: *go and make learners!*

Questions for Reflection and Conversation

1. When the idea of sharing faith is raised in your church setting, what are the concerns that emerge? To what underlying commitments do these concerns point?

2. What are you, as a member of your congregation, thinking/feeling/doing that makes it *harder* for you to share stories of faith? What would facilitate sharing of faith stories?

3. In what ways does your congregation model *ongoing regard* as an element of its faith practices?

4. Name some examples of ways a community of truth has emerged in some context of your life. Can you imagine ways that experience could become part of your faith community?

Parish Strategies

1. Spend a year with your congregation deliberately visiting them in their primary places of engagement during the week. The goal should be to listen and to collect stories of the ways in which the members' faith shapes their daily lives, and then to use those narratives as the platform for extended evangelical planning.

2. Institute a ten-minute period of time just before or after a weekly worship service when congregational members are invited to tell their own journeys of faith.

3. Have your congregational leadership write an evocative question each week based on the readings within liturgy that is then posed at the end of the liturgy (perhaps as part of the announcements) and which is also printed in the bulletin and on the Web site. Invite them to share their own responses to that question as they attend other church meetings during the week.

4. Using the resources from the *Practicing Our Faith* movement (see the Web site: www.practicingourfaith.org), invite congregation members to try some of the practices during the week. Then, when they're able, invite them to share a practice with someone.

> *Sharing the gospel with others is at the heart of learning,*
> *and hence crucial to engagement in contemporary ministry.*

10. GO AND LISTEN: REACHING OUT TO THOSE WHO SEEK— ESPECIALLY YOUNG ADULTS

Kristine A. Lund

In the last few decades, membership and attendance in the mainline denominations in North America have been declining at a steady rate. At the same time, bookstore shelves increasingly hold titles that highlight spirituality in some form or another, for example: *Purpose Driven Life: What on Earth Am I Here For?; Guardian Angels: True Stories of Answered Prayers; Course in Miracles,* and so on. A quick search on Google results in over five million sites for "spirituality" in Canada and over three million sites for "spirituality and religion." What does this mean?

While public religious behaviour, religious affiliation, and attendance have been declining, many people attach a higher degree of importance to religion than membership numbers alone would indicate. "Who's Religious,"[1] a recent study released from Statistics Canada, surveyed adult Canadians, examining their private religious practices, such as meditation, prayer, reading of sacred texts, and worship at home or some other location. Most striking was the number of people who infrequently or never attended public religious services, yet regularly engaged in personal religious practices. Of those who reported infrequently attending religious services in the year prior to the survey, 37 percent said they engaged in religious practices on their own on a weekly basis, as did 27 percent of those who never attended religious services. The study showed that religious practice was lowest among young people and that men were less likely than women to participate in religious activities.

Not surprisingly, young adults have the weakest attachment to organized religion. Even when private forms of religious behaviour are considered, almost half of Canadians ages fifteen to twenty-nine have a low frequency of religious practice. Historically, young people often abstaine from formal religious observance or Christian education for a few years. However, many return to the institutional church of their childhood when they had children of their own. While this may have been a trend in the past, it is no longer the case. Many young adults now have no inclination to expose their young children to the church of their own childhood experience. For some, this rejection of institutional religion may well be an expression of spiritual searching. To say no when grandma wants the baby baptized, at least indicates that some thought has been given to what this might mean. Who is listening to the implied questions? Who is reaching out to them, listening and engaging their questions and concerns with an evangelizing word?

The Baby Boomers' Children

Whatever our age, in order to understand the questions of today's young adults, it is important to consider their/our history, context, and stage of development. The baby boomer generation has set the context for young adults today.[2] Today's young adults are children of the baby boomer generation. Baby boomers were born in record numbers following World War II. North America was rebuilt by young couples who were dedicated to finding a good job, getting married, buying a home, and building a family. This period was one of great enthusiasm and hope. Popular culture of the time was quick to portray this optimism in songs, movies, and books.

As children, the baby boomers were seen as a privileged generation. They did not experience the Great Depression or a world war. Their childhood appeared idyllic to their parents. They were the first generation to experience television, which exposed them to programming that had simple plots and happy endings. As never before, this generation of children was encouraged to question the fundamental principles of society, and, at the same time, they were taught to value their individuality. They became the "me generation."

This idyllic childhood quickly changed when the baby boomer children became adolescents. Their secure existence was shattered with such events as the assassinations of President John F. Kennedy and Martin Luther King Jr.; the Vietnam War; and the Watergate scandal. These and other such tragic events cast a shadow on the hope and enthusiasm of this generation. Television provided much more immediate coverage of events across the globe. Never before had such information been so readily and easily accessible. Technology was burgeoning. There was increased speculation and anticipation about how science and technology would not only make lives easier, but would also provide long-sought-after answers. Music became a powerful influence, with the Beatles, Rolling Stones, and other bands and musicians performing songs that spoke to the issues of the day.

As young adults, baby boomers reshaped the way North Americans engaged their lives. Meaningful careers became more important than simply being productive. One's individuality was more significant than conforming to society's norms. Pleasure and personal fulfillment became more meaningful than contributing to the community. Acquiring possessions became a means of measuring personal and family successes. There was a shift to feeling over doing. Consequently, one's beliefs and values became individualized and, as such, allowed one to "pick-and-choose" rather than simply follow tradition. Because the baby boomer generation is so large, it has been able to significantly influence the course of North American culture. While not all boomers are alike, there seem to be a few characteristics that describe this generation. First, this generation has been able to merge free spirit idealism with moneymaking entrepreneurialism. This has resulted in a blurring of the lines between social consciousness and personal gain. Secondly, baby boomers' distrust of institutions has influenced other generations and has resulted in the development of a style of seeking that is individualistic.[3]

So, what of the generations that followed? If the baby boomers were born in a period of hope and optimism, the generations that followed have been born into a culture that has experienced continuing disillusionment in political leadership, a breakdown of the traditional family structure, and unprecedented changes in the political, social, and economic environment. This has created a very uncertain future for today's young people, including increasing costs for higher education, fewer jobs, and, for the first time, the likelihood that they will not achieve a higher standard of living than their parents. At the same time, technology has linked them to other young adults around the world, for example watching on television the massacre at Tiananmen Square, the fall of the Berlin Wall, and the terrorist attacks on the World Trade Center on September 11, 2001. Every day, world events are witnessed and vicariously participated in via the media and the Internet. Young adults are certainly pondering and questioning the meaning of all these events. These questions call the church to its ministry of education and evangelism.

Young Adults Are Younger Longer

Young children who see tragic events on television will often, in their open and innocent way, ask profound "why" questions. In some ways, it seems that children have to grow up at an ever younger age. In other ways, the emphasis in the designation young adult is on *young*. Similar to the changing experience of adolescence in the twentieth century, the stage of young adulthood in the twenty-first century is changing. The response of North American culture is ambiguous in relation to this time of life. When does adulthood arrive? Chronological age no longer serves as a predictable indicator. At one time, any of the following could indicate that a young person had reached adulthood: graduating from high school or university; obtaining a driver's license, social insurance card, or credit card; becoming sexually active; marrying; parenting a child; establishing one's own home; becoming financially independent; reaching the legal drinking age; or, becoming eligible to vote. Each of these indicators served, to some degree, as a cultural signpost of adulthood, even when the age designation varied from one region of the country to another.[4]

Things have changed. Those rites of passage no longer signify a coming-of-age. Even using an indicator for adulthood, such as "becoming established," is nebulous. Young people, even though they may be on their own, are often involved in professional education well into their thirties. At any point, they may return to their parents' home because they are burdened with student debt and/or are experiencing difficulty finding employment in their chosen field. They may change careers a number of times. They experience significant stress when what they need to know is continually changing and increasingly complex. Marriage and having children are often postponed in favor of individual pursuits.

So when does one become an adult? One could say that it is when a person is critically aware of the meaning of oneself, of others, of the world, and of God. Young adulthood is the time to ask important questions and to discover worthy dreams. These are Christian education questions. It is a time for young adults to separate themselves from the presumed truths of their childhood and adolescence and to reconstruct meaning for themselves. These are issues of discernment of what is "good news" for life. These tasks have significant consequences for the adult years to follow.

When should the young person receive the respect and trust society gives to adults? Sharon Daloz Parks, a noted author in the field of young-adult development, notes that, usually between the ages of seventeen and thirty, a particular way of meaning-making emerges that has certain adult characteristics while at the same time lacking others. This manner of making-meaning includes the development of a critical awareness of one's own reality: the ability to self-consciously engage in dialogue and the capacity to respond in ways that are satisfying and just.

Fundamental to the experience of being human is the ability to make meaning. If we are unable to make at least some sense out of things, then life is seemingly disconnected and chaotic, and we become disillusioned, confused, and distressed. Faith for today's young adults is not faith in a manner that we have traditionally understood it to be. It is not faith in a particular religious belief. Rather, faith is the process of seeking and discovering meaning in the everydayness of experience. At their core, these are Christian education and evangelism issues. In this way, faith becomes part of the larger human experience.

Popular Culture

For many young adults, meaning will be expressed in secular terms. Since many of their baby-boomer parents may have had very tenuous ties with institutional religion, Tom Beaudoin, a Catholic theologian, suggests that for the next generation it was not a large step from "religion as accessory to religion as unnecessary."[5] While the common perception may be that institutional religion, or at least the mainline churches, is slowly dying, we appear to have a popular culture that is theological in many ways. Popular songs, music videos, and movies contain much religious symbolism. Themes such as sin, salvation, grace, redemption, and many more can readily be identified in, for example, C. S. Lewis's book *The Lion, Witch and the Wardrobe* made into a movie in 2005; Mel Gibson's movie *The Passion of the Christ*; the series of Matrix movies; and the bands Never Ending Light, Evanescence, and Creed. Could it be that popular culture is the religious arena for this generation? If so, what does this mean for the church's understanding of and relationship with young adults today?

While there is disinterest and sometimes hostility towards the institutional church, young adults often claim a strong sense of spirituality in their lives. A growing number say, "I'm not religious, but I'm spiritual." There is greater ease with speaking of spirit, spirituality, or soul because these words indicate more of a personal rather than public experience. In fact, it has become quite acceptable to claim a personal spirituality, whereas being religious is seen to be less desirable.

"Organized religion kills the living beauty of God." This statement was first made by the Christian writer-philosopher Malcolm Muggeridge, but would be echoed by many young adults today. They feel they do not need an outside authority to tell them what to believe or how to live their lives. They are not looking for a community where they can find comfort in an absolute authority. They are not interested in the "ins and outs" of correct doctrine, and denominational loyalty has become less important. They are turned off by rigid doctrinal stands and seemingly unending conflict in the church on issues such as mode of baptism, women in ministry, and attitudes about lifestyle or sexual orientation. They seek a faith that will make a difference in their lives and in their community or larger world. They want results, and faith that does not tangibly improve their lives is quickly disregarded.

In order to reach out to young adults today, teachers and evangelists need to recognize the spirituality of popular culture. The spirituality of popular culture offers results and ways to get involved. Celebrities respond to various issues, for example, Bono to the crisis in Africa and Angelina Jolie to the plight of child refugees. Stephen Lewis, the UN Special Envoy for HIV/Aids in Africa repeatedly attracts large crowds of young adults whenever he addresses this issue. Pop culture provides significant information on issues such as the environmental crisis; the economic disparity among countries, as well as between groups within countries; political unrest and war. Involvement is as easy as clicking onto a Web site and indicating that you care.

Aside from living religiously through popular culture, some young adults are taking religion into their own hands, using symbols, values, and rituals from various religious traditions to create their own personal spirituality. Whether it is an interest in paganism, Eastern religions, recognition of angels in their lives, or mysticism, young adults are curious, exploring, and experimenting with a variety of spiritual expressions.

I Consume; Therefore I Am

What do we seek? This is the age-old question. It is a particularly important question in our postmodern, post-Christian, Western world. Francis Bridger, who writes in the area of pastoral theology and ethics, observes that this question also responds to two major assumptions: "Life is uncertain, fragile and this-worldly; and to consume is to live, or (to pace Descartes) 'I consume, therefore I am.'"[6] These two are not unrelated because, if life is fraught with insecurity, then it would seem appropriate to seek meaning from consuming as much as possible. In other words, the one with the most at the end wins! However, postmodern consumerism is more than one's individual accumulation of things; it is a worldview that pervades all of Western culture. It is the dominant "metanarrative."

It has been argued that consumerism is the religion of the late twentieth century and new millennium.

Craig Bartholomew, a biblical scholar, has delineated a number of characteristics that provide a framework for understanding both consumerism and the contemporary interest in spirituality. He concludes that it is important to recognize the current spiritual quest as a form of consumerism. Therefore, the values in consumerist societies are derived from consumption, rather than the other way around.

The most important value in our consumerist society is gratification. This can be physical, emotional, intellectual, spiritual, or a combination of all four. In the modern view, the spirit and the body were regarded as dual opposites. In postmodern spirituality, there is a merging of the two. From a post modern perspective, the body is a receiver of sensations and seeks experiences that provide sensations. In a consumerist culture, the individual's needs are limitless and can never be satisfied. However, this is somewhat of an irony, because while a consumerist society promises to satisfy every need, the survival of the consumerist society is founded on the premise that satisfaction can never be realized. If this is applied to the pursuit of spiritual fulfillment, it is clear that if any of the various spiritualities that claim to provide *the* answer to life's uncertainties and anxieties, they mirror the characteristics of consumerism. This is reflected in the massive proliferation of spiritual resources of every sort. In the search for spiritual fulfillment, it is the values chosen by the individual and self-created reality that are important. Since the desire for gratification is the goal behind ever-changing needs and desires, the individual's spiritual search consists of a never-ending "stream of sensation-gathering experiences."[7]

Another characteristic of consumerism is that it focuses attention on the present rather than on the past or future. This is certainly evident in the spiritual quest for the permanent "now." This should not come as a surprise given the overwhelming emphasis in Western culture on immediate gratification. For example, for many people, going shopping provides momentary satisfaction. These are false promises of the good news. To the degree that the search for spirituality is embedded in this consumerist culture, then it is expected to also provide immediate gratification. If it does not, the "shopping" continues.

In order to understand the significance of the contemporary interest in spirituality, it is important to realize that it is not only a religious phenomenon, but a sociological one as well. We are embedded—continually being educated—in a culture of consumerism, and so it is important to recognize the principles of consumerism to understand more fully the revival of interest in spirituality. We also need not to assume that this revival will automatically lead to a resurgence of religion. While it is true that there is interest in spiritual matters, it is important to not assume that evangelistic methods from the past will be useful with this generation of seekers. Recognition of our cultural context is important if we are to address the questions of young adults today.

Cyberspace

An overarching metatheme that permeates pop culture is that of virtual religiousness. Tom Beaudoin observes that young adults have developed a keen way of finding meaning in fragmentary and disparate pop-culture moments, from television commercials to music videos to styles of clothing. Meaning is very much "in the moment" and time is an "experience grasped in moments."[8]

Cyberspace can be seen as part of a "culture of moments" that originates and contributes to what Douglas Rushkoff, an author and lecturer in media theory, calls the "datasphere,"[9] that is, popular culture's massive media system of recycling stories and images." The datasphere's presence becomes evident in the way young-adult conversations are frequently "recycling images already present in the media. The datasphere includes media, fashion, cyberspace, and music videos, which are constantly being reconstructed into new meanings. The way these are variously combined means that time, meaning, and experience are bound to be "momented." Even if an individual reacts against the datasphere, they still understand themselves in relation to the datasphere. Affirmed or resisted, the datasphere has significant authority and influence in our culture. Cyberspace offers Christian educators a plethora of resources for inviting young adults into conversation. How do young adults relate to the constant stream of images that are vying for their attention? How do these images organize us in our relationship to self, to others, and to God?

Cyberspace creates an environment that is well-positioned for challenging and upsetting hierarchical institutions. Email is easily accessible, and creating a personal Web page or blog no longer requires advanced computer skills. A wide variety of topics, including those that are more socially unacceptable, can become the subject of discussion groups one can participate in from the comfort of home, the public library, or an Internet café. Technology opens up new and creative opportunities for Christian education and evangelism.

Cyberspace is a pluralistic space and, as such, could be seen as a threat to the traditional religious institution. The pluralistic nature of cyberspace challenges religion's truth claims. Someone surfing the Net can easily access information on any number of religions. This, then, raises the question of each one's relative validity or equality and gives a wider range and broader number of resources for religious belief. Whether on the Web or in the real world, young adults today are not as bound by institutions as previous generations were. Consequently, they feel freer to challenge religious institutions to clarify the uniqueness of their spiritual message and tradition. Young adults invite religious institutions to creatively rise to this challenge. We who are concerned with and involved in education as evangelism need to embrace this challenge as a welcome invitation to engage in dialogue.

If we all are to be involved in ministry with young adults today, we must be willing to enter cyberspace with all its plurality and ambiguity.[10] We need to bring a uniquely religious message to this new public forum. However, if we simply use cyberspace to reveal a church that is representative of the past, rather than one that is willing to engage the important issues of our time, young adults will find this public face of the church even less inviting. On the other hand, if we can use technology to invite young adults to consider the deep influence of culture on their spirituality and to evaluate their own spirituality as intensely as they criticize religion, then cyberspace can become a significant forum for discussion.

Go and Listen

Traditionally, evangelism has been "Go and Tell," modeled on the Great Commission of Matthew 28. Many young adults today are not open to this style of delivering the gospel message. As noted previously, they are suspicious of the institutional church and view it as a rigid, "dogmafied" structure that has nothing to offer. In his ministry, Jesus used things that were common to the context to engage his audience: a grain of wheat, the mustard seed, sheep and goats, and so on. In order to attract this current generation, the church needs to find ways to engage that which is common for young adults, that is, popular culture. The church has often set itself over against popular culture, believing that it needed to be protected from such influences. Yet the life of Jesus reminds us that God became human and entered into a particular cultural context, meeting and responding to the needs of those he encountered. This is the challenge for the church today. How can we enter into our current cultural context, be open to engage those we meet and listen to what it is they are searching for?

Many of us may find listening can be difficult when our beliefs, values, and ways of being religious are challenged. We may feel threatened. We may worry that if our answers to these questions do not address the needs of the young, perhaps our answers will be called into question for us as well. This is our fear and is not something we necessarily welcome. Those of us who are young adults need to know that we are not the only ones grappling with the larger questions of life. Perhaps, in the midst of our fears, there is a place for younger, middle-aged and older adults to meet, recognizing that we all search for meaning in the midst of a chaotic and unsettled world.

While it is not easy to be challenged, such experiences also offer us opportunities to see ourselves in ways that we could not envision on our own. For example, I have had an opportunity to teach in another country. I was initially surprised to hear how people responded to my being Canadian and their perceptions of Canada and North America as a whole. Not all of their perceptions were easy to hear, but I learned a lot about myself as a Canadian when seen through others' eyes.

Many young adults experience the church as not living with integrity, seeing the church preaching one message and living out another within the community. For example: "They say everyone's welcome, but I'm gay, or poor, or have a ring through my nose or a tattoo on my arm; they avoid my gaze and I don't feel welcome." Likewise, young adults challenge the church to evaluate its structure and ask whether we are an evolving or fixed institution. Young adults call the church back to its roots as a "reforming church." We are called to live in the midst of inherent instability, recognizing that to be a "reforming church" means to be a church constantly in flux and therefore vulnerable. Paradoxically accepting our own fleeting existence means being willing to make the institution's future secondary, focusing, rather, on the heart of the gospel message. If churches speak authentically from a position of vulnerability and not from a belief in a divine entitlement to preach, they can model that transience does not necessarily mean spiritual irrelevance. For young adults who are so immersed in a temporary culture, this could be a welcome message to hear.

Many young adults are not in the church because they claim that so little there relates directly to their world or experience. In the vacuum created by their absence, the church seems at a loss in knowing how to respond. When this period of life is ignored or merely seen as a time of transition, a significant opportunity is lost. One possibility for the church might be in the area of mentoring. The arena of cyberspace provides us with the unique opportunity to meet and mentor young people, known to us or not, even though they have not yet or not recently come through any church doors. Cyberspace is the world of young adults, one where they feel comfortable and move around with ease. Over the Internet, young adults have the opportunity to enter discussions anonymously, allowing them to be more open about themselves given the "distance" between participants. In other words, this technology supports young adults in asking questions and discussing religious topics in a way that is sometimes easier for them than face-to-face conversations. Cyberspace also allows young adults who have had a difficult experience or no experience with the church a safe and convenient way to participate.

Cyberspace can also offer opportunities for community that can augment the traditional face-to-face community. The church can use this virtual space to build and maintain community when ministering to young adults. There are also some young adults who want to participate in a solitary manner. Cyberspace offers a way to engage with religious questions while never engaging the community further. Many religious and spiritual resources exist online: Bibles, reference guides, and commentaries. However, this is also a place where the church could provide study resources, links to relevant Web sites, and opportunities to be involved at arm's length.

For those interested, cyberspace offers many opportunities for getting involved in social action. For example, it is possible to contribute funds to a variety of aid projects, such as assisting the victims of a natural disaster or the global AIDS/HIV crisis. One can participate in environmental action groups and letter-writing campaigns. Virtual communities can be experienced as real as those that meet face-to-face. The church needs to meet young adults here. Young adults want to make a difference, and they want their faith to be relevant. By using technology, churches have the opportunity to facilitate young adults in integrating their life and faith.

Cyberspace is a reminder that, as humans, we live a limited and bounded existence. It is impossible for us to know everything. In fact, I am just one person in the midst of millions in cyberspace, exploring a minute fraction of what is out there. So, while we experience our limits, we also have a taste of the infinite. We yearn for the divine to be present in our current reality. This is the challenge of education and evangelism. For many young adults, cyberspace is a place where spirituality and present life meet.

Questions for Reflection and Conversation

1. Where does faith and technology intersect in your life? What ways have you found to use technology to support or enhance your faith?

2. How is popular culture reflected in your congregation's worship?

3. What is exciting about using more technology in the life of the church?

4. How do you see the Lutheran Church as a "reforming church?" How might we invite young adults to be part of the ongoing reformation?

Parish Strategies

1. Develop a list of email addresses for young adults that you know. Begin to communicate with them using email to connect, inform them of church activities that might interest them, and invite discussion about issues or topics.

2. Invite a young adult who is not active in your congregation out for lunch or coffee. Primarily go as a listener. Hear what is important in their lives. What are the questions or issues that they are struggling with? What is it like for them to be maturing into adulthood in this context?

3. Develop a mentoring program within the congregation.

4. Identify projects in your community in which you or other young adults can become involved. Invite them to participate in responding to a need in your community.

5. Develop the church Web page to include links to other organizations, institutions, or resources.

> *For many young adults, cyberspace is a place*
> *where spirituality and life meet.*

11. LEARN TO SHARE CHRIST IN THE LANGUAGES OF PEOPLE'S DAILY LIVES

Norma Cook Everist

"We cannot keep from speaking about what we have seen and heard." So said Peter and John (Acts 4:20). God had used them to heal a lame man, and they taught the amazed crowds about this God who gives life. For this, they got into trouble, were taken into custody and questioned, and ordered not to speak or teach at all in the name of Jesus. But they would not be silent!

In the midst of our ministry in daily life, we are and will be called into question for the ministry we do and be called to give witness to the hope that lies within us. Education that is real and alive leads to evangelism, and evangelism leads to the need for more education. Sharing the faith needs to be done in the languages people speak all week long. Once in a while, someone will simply be passing by the church on a Sunday morning and walk in. Once in a while, the quoting of a random Bible passage will bring a person to faith. But only once in a while. Most of the time, we need to reach out and intentionally meet people where they are. In order to do this, we need to speak their languages, listen carefully to their needs, and be able to speak of God's great love in direct relation to their human need.

Peter and John were able to put into words the ministry they were doing and boldly say in whose name they were acting. They knew the Christ in whose name they ministered. We, too, need to know Christ well. If Christians do not understand the biblical and theological grounding of their faith, they may resort to using mere moralistic tidbits and biblical clichés. We need more than a cliché. Jesus walked where people walked. He often asked, "What do you want me to do for you?" He called self-righteousness and legalistic judgment for what it was: playing God, not ministry. Sharing Christ at the workplace is not effective evangelism when it is merely an assumption that everyone at the worksite or in the world should be "a Christian, just like me." Likewise, simplistic religious slogans pass right by a person's real need. To learn the faith and to share the faith in the languages of people's daily lives enhances the effectiveness of both education and evangelism.

Certainly Laity Sunday can be a significant event. Ministry of the laity, however, is not primarily about letting a lay person preach, but rather about lifting up the varieties of vocations the baptized people of God engage in all week long. This means giving attention all year long to equipping all Christians educationally for sharing the gospel in words that connect to people where they are. A number of chapters in this book have pointed out the necessity of helping people connect their faith with daily life in order for education and evangelism to be connected. To take it one step further, it is not a question of convincing people to speak/preach/proclaim, but first of all seeing what it is people are already proclaiming in the daily conversations. Do people understand the faith undergirding the decisions they are making? And are they making decisions that promote justice?

So often what we learn on Sunday is disconnected from what we talk about all week. Not that we want to disconnect, but we do not know how to put it together. But if we begin in the languages of daily life, we may be able to translate God's word into the vernacular, into ordinary terms, images, and vocabulary, so that we can be the evangelizing disciples of God. Many Christians feel more confident and willing to translate God's love into action than into words. When people are equipped to speak in their natural languages, they become more skilled with words . . . and, like Peter and John, more willing to speak of what they "have seen and heard."

Education and Evangelism as a Translating Experience

Educators know the importance of honoring diverse learning styles. People begin their learning most effectively when they can use their native tongue. When a person's first language, and the culture surrounding it, is honored, people have a sense of self-worth that enhances their ability to learn more languages. Children especially have a marvelous ability to learn a second, or even a third, language. French and English are the two official languages of Canada; people benefit from being able to communicate in both. English-only speakers in the United States are at a distinct disadvantage globally, and also in their own communities, in being able to communicate with and learn from people different from themselves.

How do we meet people? We honor the people we meet by respecting their language. When we are in a land where people speak a language we do not know, we can try to learn as much as we can, at least common greetings. Such openness says, "I want to know you. You know things I do not know. I want to learn from you." In carefully listening to one another, we connect in a whole new way.

So, too, one's willingness to listen and learn from someone speaking their "Monday language," not their Sunday faith-tradition language, says, "I honor who you are and believe that God is present in your weekday life." By really wanting to know about the person's life and their world views, we connect with them.

Surely people need to learn about the stories, concepts, and truths about God from the Scriptures, the language of the liturgy and the confessions of the church. Biblical illiteracy and ignorance about church history and theology undermines the life and mission of a congregation. Martin Luther was convinced that people should be able to read the Scriptures for themselves and to worship and pray in the vernacular, the common language of the people. The importance of his translating the New Testament into the vernacular cannot be underestimated. How do we help people read the Scriptures and help them let the Scriptures "read them" in regard to the issues they face all week long? How can we help people translate the Bible and the theology of the church into phrases and concepts that prepare them to think, feel, relate, and make decisions in the languages they speak all week?

Once people are able to conceptualize the faith in the common parlance of family, work, and leisure activities, they will be able to more naturally talk about God in those places. We need to develop a healthy rhythm of being the gathered people of God for worship and for education and the scattered people of God for mission and ministry in daily life.[1] In order to do that, both places need to be translating experiences. Our Christian education can help people learn the biblical and theological heritage of the faith and help them connect this faith to daily life. Likewise, education for evangelism includes helping Christians listen carefully to the languages the people they meet speak in their daily lives and understand the real needs of people. Once people know they have permission to use those languages and to make those connections, they will never again *not* make such connections; they will become more effective evangelizers in the broadest sense of that term. This does not mean trying to make over the workplace into their own version of Christianity, nor shape the global society into an image of their own country; that's simply a new form of colonialism. It does mean being able to share the love of Christ in a language people can understand. So how do we give people permission to learn in the vernacular?

Jan had been a forest ranger in the Rocky Mountains. She was invited to bring that experience into a congregational workshop on leadership development for new council members. At first, Jan was quiet, even reluctant to speak. Through being encouraged to speak using the terminology of her background, she became very articulate. She spoke about the importance of planning. "When you know you are going out in the morning in fire season, the challenge is great. Others depend upon your leadership for their very lives. You need flexibility, but you can't simply decide you will make those plans when you get there. You need to have everything ready beforehand." Her insights were valuable, and she was able to translate them appropriately to the task of leadership in the congregation.

Al was a roofer for a local Midwestern construction firm. He saw things other people did not. He always noticed the pitch of a roof, how it could face the elements. That information might seem irrelevant to some, but it was crucial information for his ministry in daily life. And once people showed an interest in his arena of daily life, he began speaking that language in an adult education forum. He spoke of a "sheltering" God. And others could listen to him and see his perceptions of God through the lens of his eyes, even while they might have different lenses.

Languages People Speak

So what languages do people in your community speak?

When asked what languages were spoken in arenas of daily life, the people in just one faith community responded with the following: (They have been categorized in terms of "vocation," "relationships," "location," and "outlook.")

Vocation:

Music, Nursing, Agriculture, Youth, Education, Scouting, Health Care/Wellness, Academia, Business, Architecture, Sports, Law Enforcement, Computer Technology, Electronics, Engineering, Grocery Retail, Fishing, Social Work, Gardening, Clothing Design, Therapy, Psychiatry, Volunteer Boards/Committees, Construction, Cooking, Management, Real Estate, Developmental Disabilities, Art, Woodworking, Military, Optometry, Geriatrics, Environment, Student, Politics, Factory Work, Banking, Customer Service.

Relationships:

Family, Mother, Father, Grandparent, Son/Daughter, Spouse (including the vocational language of the spouse), Mentor, Patient, Commuter, "Guy talk," Alcoholics Anonymous

Location (Genre)

Midwestern, Southern Rural, Hometown, Metropolitan, Small City, Native American, Outdoors/Camping, Nature, Church, Fifties, Surf.

Outlook

Humor, Simplicity, Melancholy, Sarcasm, Quest, Laughter, Tears, Imagination, Discernment, Passion

People in other faith communities would come up with different responses to the question, "What languages do you speak?" What was remarkable, and somewhat surprising, was that everyone was able to answer the question without prodding (after making clear that this was not about languages in the usual sense of the word, that is, Spanish, German, Swahili). The question was open ended. The responses given here named "outlook" were not asked for nor anticipated. Some just decided to give that kind of a response. It was the language in which they thought, conceptualized, and spoke.

Articles of Faith

Beyond their languages of everyday life, Christians who hold the same faith speak a common creed using the same words. The historic creeds, the Apostles' and Nicene, are confessed together in Sunday worship.

The Apostles' Creed Article 1: I believe in God the Father Almighty, Creator of Heaven and Earth.

The God whom we confess creates not only "me," but all that exists. Cultural beliefs focus on a God whose job, we presume, is to protect me, *my* family, *my* job, *my* church, *my* country. Rather, in this article, a faith community, together with Christians around the globe and through the ages, confesses that they fear, love, and trust in the Triune God above all things. Saying "I," but also looking around at all these other believers (it is a creed, not a prayer—it's okay to look around), we confess that this God is the Creator, the Protector, and the Provider of *all*.

The words people confess on Sunday need to ground their lives comprehensively all week long. How people translate the meaning, as well as their interpretations of these words, has significant consequences in the decisions they make in the arenas of their ministries in daily life. In every dimension of life, one needs to ask, "What is God creating here? How is God providing? Just whom is God protecting?"

The educating faith community will help people raise questions about this God, who is almighty and the creator of all. Where do people stand on the issue of creationism? Immigration? How do one's Christian beliefs relate to capitalism? Consumerism? Globalization? Economic justice? The people among whom we minister, whom we lead to be disciples in the world, live inside all of those systems and both benefit from them and oppress others by them. The issues are large, the choices complex. Parishioners and the people they meet in their daily lives have choices: whom to hire and fire, how to get out from under credit-card debt, how to care for children when there has been a divorce. How do you care about people still suffering from hurricanes here and from earthquakes half a world away? What does it really mean to believe in a creating, providing, protecting God?

Article 2: I believe in Jesus Christ, God's only Son, our Lord. He was conceived by the power of the Holy Spirit and born of the Virgin Mary. He suffered under Pontius Pilate, was crucified, died and was buried. He descended into hell. On the third day he rose again. He ascended into heaven and is seated at the right hand of the Father. He will come again to judge the living and the dead.

Jesus Christ draws the faith community into the streets, where ordinary people live and work. So, too, our teaching is not confined to the classroom. It needs to equip people for their roles and relationships in ministry opportunities on the streets, in the corporate boardrooms, at the medical center, wherever they go all week long. Who is this Jesus Christ in whose name we teach? Where did Christ walk? Or maybe the question is, "Is there anywhere Christ did not walk?"

Incarnational ministry is a ministry of presence, real presence, an active presence that reaches out to engage people in their real-life ministry settings, whether dramatic or mundane. This calls for biblical and theological teaching that can help people translate the death and resurrection of Christ into liberating, life-giving ministry. It may begin with an encounter on the streets. Encounters can lead to engagements which can lead to evangelization. In saying we believe that Christ was conceived by the Holy Spirit and born of Mary, we confess the power of the Spirit at work through human beings; we believe Christ was incarnate, put on flesh and lived among all kinds of people, proclaiming God's reign and caring, healing, and calling for justice. His death and resurrection defeated oppressive forces of sin, Satan, and death itself. We confess that the One who rose from the dead and ascended is still incarnate.

We might ask, along with Mary, what in the world God is calling us to give birth to? What are the oppressive, death-delivering powers that need new life? And how is Christ present in the world today so that all might be united in God's love forever? To believe in Jesus Christ is to fully encounter and engage the world and its people and to minister with the good news of Christ's life-giving power.

Article 3: I believe in the Holy Spirit, the holy catholic church, the communion of saints, the forgiveness of sins, the resurrection of the body and the life everlasting.

What makes people holy? What does it mean to confess together that one believes in the Holy Spirit? The Holy Spirit brings individuals and whole communities to faith and, after disillusionment, back to faith again and again. Ministry is rooted in the forgiveness of sins. Life everlasting is not just a ticket to heaven, but new life in Christ lived in community as the body of Christ now.

The Spirit transforms entire communities for ministries in daily life. And those ministries are diverse. The various callings of different people in a faith community may take them in opposite directions culturally, economically, or politically. No matter. As the community gathers each time at the communion table, they are restored, strengthened, and empowered to go forth and serve in the world as one body of Christ with many members. As they gather for rich, relative, and relational Christian education, they are equipped to be the holy people who are not afraid to become involved in the dirt and grime of what may seem like unholy work.

Teachers and leaders who are charged to walk with and equip people for their ministries in daily life may say, "I already have too much to do now." However, to believe in the communion of saints is to believe that God is the Creator of the whole world and that Christ is already and continues to be incarnate in that world, and to claim the Spirit's power. As educators walk with the laity, listen to and engage the theological questions people raise while trying to make sense of it all, ministerial teaching may become more interesting, more vital, more theologically challenging and alive.

On Pentecost, people from many nations came together. The disciples "were all together in one place" and were "filled with the Holy Spirit and began to speak in other tongues, as the Spirit gave them utterance." The amazing message of Pentecost is that the people who had come to Jerusalem all heard, in their own languages, what the disciples were saying. They were bewildered, amazed, and wondering, but they heard! The good news of the Spirit is that the Spirit enables us, too, to speak the good news in languages that people can hear about Jesus Christ. "We hear them telling in our own tongues the mighty works of God" (Acts 2:11).

Good News for the Human Predicament

So what is the connection between the creeds that we confess and education as evangelism? By believing in a creating, providing, protecting God; in the incarnate, risen Christ; and in the Spirit, disciples are empowered to speak about Christ in languages people can understand. The good news is not good news if it is not specifically related to the needs of people, the human predicament. Theologian Letty Russell wrote that Jesus did not say to a blind person, "You can walk," nor to a person who could not walk, "You can see."[2] Christ looked right at a person and asked, "What do you want me to do for you?" Jesus cared about people and the societal problems related to human need.

In exploring the various aspects of the human predicament and in listening carefully to people tell about the issues they really face, we begin to understand that each person is an individual. Giving *my* witness, telling *my* story, is not sufficient. A bumper sticker reads, "If Jesus is the answer, what is the question?" Well, what *is* the question? What is the specific human need, the basic problem, the human predicament? Christian discipleship is not just passing the one-question exam with the general answer, "Jesus." It is speaking the good news in each person's language according to each person's need.

Jesus died one death for all, but that "all" includes real people in differing situations. If the human problem is guilt, the good news is that God through Jesus Christ forgives. If the human problem is brokenness, the good news is that Jesus makes us whole. If the human problem is alienation, the good news is that God reconciles and restores relationships. If the human problem is being lost, the good news is that the Good Shepherd looks for and finds the lost. If the human problem is death, Jesus Christ has brought new life. If the human problem is judgment, the good news in Jesus Christ is unconditional acceptance. If the human problem is bondage, the good news is Jesus brings freedom.[3] If the human problem is emptiness, Jesus Christ fills life with new callings to use one's gifts. If the human problem is being overwhelmed by the stress and demands of daily life, Jesus invites the weary to come to him and to rest in the caring arms of the God who, alone, is able to guide.

Fran's problem is not one of feeling guilty. Telling her, "You are forgiven," would not phase her. She is wrapped up in her obsession with compulsive buying. For Martin Luther, the basic human predicament—sin—is idolatry. Unable to trust in God the Provider, she is, of course, guilty of idolatry. But how do we meet Fran where she is? She is not unlike many people whose working theology is, "In debt we trust." Is Fran's predicament at core a feeling of lack of self-worth? Does she need to know of what great worth she is to God and to those around her? The evangelizing disciple will need to learn astute skills in just how to reach Fran with the good news of Jesus Christ.

Keith's deep, recurring problem is fear of abandonment. Whether it was in school years ago, in his profession today, or in his relationships, there remains from his childhood trauma a sense that he is lost and may never be truly found. He does not need to hear, "Get a life!" To love Keith with the gospel is to be with him in his fear of abandonment. Through empathetic accompaniment, he may be able to hear that Christ experienced the ultimate abandonment on the cross, "God, why have you forsaken me?" (Mark 15:34) and that through Christ's resurrection, God's love will never abandon Keith.

Malcolm, a man of great faith, may be one of the most free of all men, even though he lives his daily life in bondage in the prison system. He longs to be with his family. Glib words, "All things work together for good for those who love Jesus," would not only be inappropriate, but cruel. However, Malcolm *is* convinced that in Jesus Christ, nothing "will be able to separate us from the love of God in Christ Jesus our Lord" (Rom. 8:39). He thrives on letters that remind him of that which he already deeply believes, that Jesus Christ is present with him in prison and frees and empowers him to minister where he is. And minister he does, to other men in prison, through Bible study, giving pastoral care to men going through a hard time, teaching them about Jesus. Malcolm has learned and continues to grow in Christ. He is an educated evangelist.

A Four-Stage Approach

One needs to inquire about the people one is teaching. Who are the people among whom we are called to teach? What languages do they speak? How do we teach them?

And lest we stop at assessing our own teaching skills, how does our teaching help them grow in faith? How are they interpreting what they hear? Is it being received as good news?

Furthermore, we need to move beyond the church doors and inquire about arenas in daily life where congregants carry out their mission and ministry. How are they translating the good news into languages that people speak there? How are they growing in discipleship through the very process of being disciples?

Our educational ministry reaches even further. How are the people among whom the congregation members work and minister hearing the gospel these disciples live and speak? How does what we teach actually impact those people and their lives, individually and collectively? How is the gospel at work in the world?

In exploring answers to those questions, various people's real stories unfold in the following four-stage approach. Not all the stories are mentioned in each of the four sections below. The scenarios of their lives move in and out through the paragraphs, periodically and in random order, as do the scenes of our own lives and those of the people among whom we minister.

1. Who are the people among whom we are called to teach? What languages do they speak?

Mark speaks the language of "musician." A percussionist, he has taught individual students, age five through college level. Within the field of music, Mark says, "I speak different 'dialects,' Bach, Beethoven, Pink Floyd, Springsteen, different genres." He says he also speaks parent and child, as he is both a son and a father as well as a husband.

Sue is a nurse. She is fluent in the language of "health" and "medications." Medical language has a lot of sublanguages, for example "medical emergency," "intensive care," "outpatient."

Tom is a farmer and a mechanic. He describes himself as a hands-on learner. He said he never memorized a manual because it was soon out of date. He speaks "varied agriculture" and "rural America." He also knows some medical language because he is an emergency medical technician (EMT).

Miriam teaches piano, is an artist, and an editor. She is also a graduate student. She likes to ask questions and have people ask questions of her. She said, "I speak many languages: music, art, mom, grandma, publishing."

Lang Li is a university chaplain. She likes the company of university students as she helps them go through struggles and dream about their futures. She helps them seek not only answers, but questions. She speaks Taiwanese, Chinese, and English, *and* she speaks the "language of university student" in various countries and cultures.

What would it be like to visit these people in the arenas of their daily lives? How much might we learn? How might we honor them by learning at least some phrases of their languages? How might we encourage them to speak their daily languages as they pray and as they study scripture in relationship to life? By encouraging them in adult education experiences at church to "translate" as they go along, they will more quickly and more easily see how faith is relevant for them and, in turn, for their ministries.

2. How are people interpreting what they hear? How is our teaching helping people grow in faith? Is it being received as good news?

"I'm an auditory learner," said Jason. "I remember what I hear, especially the inflection of the voice. I teach English to people who speak languages other than English, and I listen hard." In his own learning, Jason interprets teaching and preaching from the Bible not only through the words used, but by peoples' expressions. Jason has lived most of his life under parental judgment. He will know if he is hearing words preached or taught in a judgmental tone or in genuine acceptance and forgiveness.

"I'm a cognitive type. I drafted 'how-to' manuals in the legal field on how to process immigrants," said Michelle. Knowing how she learns and how she shares what she learns helps Michelle clarify how she will minister and how she will share the good news through her work and words. "Teach me and then stay with me," says Michelle.

Left on their own, people have the propensity to change Gospel into Law, to reduce the good news about Jesus Christ to mere moralisms. Michelle *could* read the Scriptures as a "how-to manual." But the God of steadfast love bids us to teach in such way that Michelle will experience a caring faith community that not only teaches, but stays with her as she grows in faith. This key difference determines whether education will be an evangelizing experience for Michelle.

Music continues to be very important for Mark, the percussionist mentioned above. But his most serious questions these days relate to his role as a father. He says that, through solid biblical study, "My love for Holy Scriptures has changed from a closed, literalistic understanding to a much more open, living, collaborative, Sprit-filled process."

Tom, the farmer and mechanic, says, "It has been my goal to integrate my life and my faith; this has been incredibly difficult for me."

Lang Li notes that at the university, "Some voices are actively silenced, or at least the students perceive that their questions are suppressed. Suppress the language and you oppress the people." She adds, "I can remember thinking about my own learning, 'If I don't have this language in my head; I cannot give it voice.'"

3. Beyond the church door, where do people who have been learning the faith go all week to carry out their mission and ministry? How are they translating the good news into languages that people speak there? How are they growing in discipleship through the very process of being disciples?

Sue, the nurse, often needs to speak with people about things they don't want to talk about, helping people understand a language they cannot conceptualize. She said, "I have an ability to discuss things in a language people can understand, to break it down in components." Her ministry is challenging. The need is clear. In the midst of the pain of life, Christ the healer is there. Sue is convinced of that, even when physical cure is beyond reach.

As Mark's sons grow and change, what is his calling so that they may become young men of faith with gifts of their own to share in the world? His study of Scripture as a more open, collaborative, Spirit-filled process is shaping his way of interacting with his sons in his ministry as a father.

Jason, who teaches English to those new to the country says, "I hear what two people are saying and they aren't connecting, so I'm a bridge. My growing edge is to help them reach across and not do it for them."

Miriam, a relatively young, vivacious woman, suffered a stroke. This woman who "spoke so many languages" of music, art, publishing, and more, now struggles to communicate at all. The reality she faces is daunting. Feelings of despair and abandonment would not be surprising. Simplistic words about Jesus making all things better would not do. But trusting in the Christ who faced the loneliness and helplessness of the cross, and surrounded by people who steadfastly love her, she continues to experience God's presence. Through the months in the hospital and, later, at a rehabilitation center, Miriam ministered powerfully, "speaking" of God's steadfast love with her eyes. And people have "seen and heard" the good news. Now at home with her parents after months of work, she is re-learning words and, with her left hand, she is drawing again and playing duets on the piano with her mother.

Tom would like to be in farming full time, but finances dictate that his mechanical skills are what mostly earn him a living today. The arenas of his daily life are the same; he sees many of the same people, but his role and relationship with them has changed. Sometimes he feels bitter, even embarrassed. But more than he may know, Tom relates well to others. Supported by members of his congregation, Tom is encouraged that he is ministering to people. He also wants to learn how to be an evangelical witness through his words.

4. How are the people among whom the congregation members work and minister hearing the gospel these disciples live and speak? How does what we teach actually impact those people and their lives, individually and collectively? How is the gospel at work in the world?

Michelle, who drafted how-to manuals, through mutual learning and accountability within her faith community, has broadened her concept of what her vocation might be. Since her own Christian education has been an evangelizing experience, she is now helping the congregation understand the complicated issues of immigration. She wants to help the congregation stay with new immigrants as they become part of the local community.

Tom wants to translate the gospel into meaning in people's daily lives. Not only is he a hands-on learner, but his ministry is also very concrete. Through being able to talk about his ministry within the faith community, Tom is coming to see that the people among whom he ministers as a mechanic, and especially through his tending people as an EMT, *do* receive the ministry of Christ through his hands. While he had a hard time integrating his faith and life abstractly, he is able to integrate it when he starts telling about Christ at work in people's lives.

Jason has recently begun to realize that not everyone is burdened with lifelong feelings of being judged, as he is. In fact, some of those for whom he is trying to be a bridge seem oblivious to a God of righteousness and unconcerned about anyone beyond themselves. In order to be an evangelizing minister, he will need to speak a prophetic word about economic injustice in the world and God's will for distributive justice. He also knows how to not *be* judge of those among whom he ministers, but to help them hear about Christ in a way that they can begin to make the connections and themselves be bridges in the world.

Sue has used her language and experience in health care to work with others who speak these languages to design and develop an interfaith parish nurse program in her city. It is thriving today. She adds that she also uses her background to guide people in their biblical journey: "Together we learn and grow a deeper understanding of God in our daily lives. Without patience and perseverance, we may well become discouraged. Teaching is being kind, patient, compassionate, and engaged with people." This is good news.

Questions for Reflection and Conversation

1. What "languages" do people in your congregation speak in their arenas of daily life?

2. How might current educational ministry offerings more fully utilize experiences from people's daily life? What educational methods might facilitate this?

3. What are the joys and struggles, the ethical issues, and decisions that people of faith face in daily life? What does the gospel have to say to each of those?

4. How can your faith community work at helping people translate the basics of the faith in conversations they have with ordinary people they encounter in ways that help them meet Christ?

Parish Strategies

1. As a congregational team, walk (drive) around your parish neighborhood and simply observe and listen. What is the good news that is needed there?

2. Arrange to visit a few parishioners in the arenas of their daily lives. Ask them to tell you, in their language, what is happening there? (This could be linked to Parish Strategy 1 in chapter 9.) What is God doing there? Then, invite and equip a few more people to make these accompaniment visits. Together, talk about what you learn and where you can go next with education as evangelism.

> *Education that is real and alive leads to evangelism,*
> *and evangelism leads to the need for more education.*

12. REDEDICATE OURSELVES TO OUR CALLING IN EDUCATION: A SOCIAL STATEMENT

Susan Wilds McArver

The chapters in this book make convincing cases for the connection between evangelism and education. In this final chapter, we return to the question raised in chapter one, namely, what do we mean exactly when we use the term *education*? We may feel that we know instinctively what education is. It is schooling. It is teaching. It is training. It is the passing on of knowledge from one person to another. Diane Hymans wrote about formation, nurture, and discipleship. While it is certainly all of these things, is it also more.

Between 2003 and 2007, the Evangelical Lutheran Church in America (ELCA) struggled intentionally with these very questions of definition. This chapter serves as a case study, examining the experience of one mainline denomination as it drew on the resources of its theological tradition and core beliefs in an attempt to come to an understanding of a subject that, initially, seemed straightforward, but in the end, turned out to be much more complex than anticipated.

Background

In 2001, the ELCA Churchwide Assembly called on the church to initiate a process to create a social statement on the subject of education. In the ELCA, social statements are not binding directives to which all of the faithful must subscribe. Rather, they serve as theological and teaching documents, designed to assist individual members and the church at large to make thoughtful and faithful choices as they consider important social issues. Since the formation of the ELCA in 1988, the Division for Church in Society has overseen the development of eight social statements on topics as diverse as health and health care, abortion, the death penalty, and the environment. All of these documents serve not only to guide individuals in their daily lives, but also to guide the institutional life and policy of the larger church.[1]

The creation of any ELCA social statement involves a multistep process. The Division for Church in Society appoints a task force composed of people who bring together the diverse gifts and backgrounds needed for consideration of the task at hand. Task forces meet several times over a period of years to consider issues, share insights, draw on experts, and conduct hearings throughout the larger church in order to gain the knowledge and information needed for their assignment.

Out of this preliminary work, the task force may then create a study document for consideration and discussion by various groups throughout the church. Individual church members, congregations, institutions, agencies, and churchwide staff are invited to contribute their thoughts to the next steps of the process based on review of the study document.

After the review process, the task force then creates the first draft of the actual social statement itself. As with the study document, the task force circulates the first draft throughout the church for discussion, feedback, and suggestions from as many constituencies as possible. Based on the response to this first draft, the task force then writes the actual proposed statement, which still faces a concluding review process as it makes its way to the Church Council and then to the Churchwide Assembly for final approval or reconsideration.

The process stands as a lengthy, even cumbersome, one, but one deliberately devised to obtain as much careful thought and response as possible from the church at large in order to obtain the best thinking available on any given topic. As it proceeds, the process in and of itself proves an educational one for the church.

The ELCA Social Statement on Education

In the particular case of the ELCA Social Statement on Education, the Division for Church in Society appointed a task force in February of 2003. This task force met for the first time in July 2003. The group members came from all across the church's life. The sixteen participants included college, university, and seminary professors; public-school educators and administrators; Lutheran day-school administrators; a community-college instructor; a college student; a bishop; a lay person who is an astronomer; and several ordained pastors. Additional advisors serving the task force throughout the process included representatives from the Division for Ministry (renamed and restructured during the course of the study as the Vocation and Education Unit), the Church in Society unit, and ELCA staff consultants from the areas of Public Policy, Christian Education, and Augsburg Fortress Publishing, eventually bringing to twenty-five the number involved in the development of the statement.

Two issues emerged in the earliest meetings of the task force. First, the diversity of the group proved, at least in the beginning, to be both its greatest strength and its largest challenge. Members of the task force came from such a wide variety of backgrounds that they sometimes found it difficult simply to talk with each other. Practitioners of public policy, science, and educational administration proved to speak quite different "languages" from each other, languages that were also different from those spoken by theologians, seminary professors, and pastors. Often, in the earliest meetings, members had to stop and ask for clarification of terminology and meaning in an honest attempt at mutual understanding and commitment to the work.

But what also became quickly apparent in the early meetings proved even more fundamental: those gathering to consider writing a social statement on education had very different ideas on exactly what such a social statement should include. Indeed, the most basic question to be answered in those early meetings was: What exactly do we mean by the term *education*?

The original 2001 motion passed by the ELCA Churchwide Assembly that had propelled the formation of the social statement forward asked that the ELCA develop a statement "that addresses the numerous accomplishments and concerns of education in the United States and its territories," recognizing that the church "is committed to justice for all," while noting that "a correlation exists between education and poverty."[2]

By the time the task force met for the first time in July 2003, the Board of the Division for Church in Society had more specifically provided guidelines for the social statement and asked the task force to produce a document that would:

- present a Lutheran vision of education for our time
- address issues of education and schooling for children and young people in our society, with attention to purpose and quality, equity and access for all, responsibilities, and religion's role in public schooling
- set forth an understanding of our church's own educational institutions (preschool, primary, and secondary schools, and colleges and universities)
- consider our church's ministries in relation to public schools and universities and the vocation of those involved in education in different roles[3]

From the start, however, some on the task force began to question this definition of education and the defined scope of the proposed study. While those attending the first meeting spent most of their time discussing issues related to public policy and public schooling, it quickly became apparent that other issues waited at the table for consideration.

Education is often equated with a system of teaching that prepares young people for productive work in the society, for citizenship in the nation, or for both. But does education refer only to what happens in public and private school settings? Does it concern only that which happens in institutional settings from preschool to the university? Is the church's concern for education visible only when it is asked to speak through its institutions on issues of public policy regarding the education of persons for work in the world?

In an attempt to come to some agreement on this most basic issue, the task force began with the fundamentals: scripture and the heritage of its Lutheran tradition.

Scripture and Tradition

From their origins as a denomination in the sixteenth century, Lutherans have historically prized education. Lutheranism itself was born at Wittenberg University, where Dr. Martin Luther served as a professor of Bible. It proved natural, therefore, for the task force to begin its work with a study of the theological and biblical bases for its work.[4]

The task force grounded its commission in the belief that "God cares for and governs all of life, including education . . . [and that] education is a human activity through which God blesses individuals and society."[5] While recognizing that it is through "faith in the gospel—not our works or our education—[that] people are reconciled to God and called into the Church,"[6] the task force affirmed that "as part of God's good but still fallen creation, human beings are given the ability to know their world," though in a way that is necessarily "incomplete and partial and often distorted." Christians are called, stated the task force, "to share the opportunities of education and bear responsibilities for education for the common good and the care of creation."[7]

As a university professor, Luther's study of the Bible eventually led him to his revolutionary understandings of scripture, understandings he felt called to share with the world. His "reformation discovery" that "the just shall live by grace through faith" was in every way a theological discovery. But it had implications far beyond the esoteric walls of the theological ivory tower. Luther's reading of scripture carried enormous social, political, and even economic consequences that Luther could hardly have foreseen. In an unexpected domino effect, many of the natural consequences of his theology spun out to influence everything from national boundaries to the German language to marriage and family life.

One of the more far-reaching results of the Reformation came from Luther's simple redefinition of the term, *vocation*. Then, as now, vocation tended in most minds to have a fairly specific and narrow connotation. In the sixteenth century, vocation held a strictly religious meaning: to take up a religious vocation meant to enter into a monastic order. In the twenty-first century, in contrast, the term vocation normally connotes something entirely secular: paid work or, in some instances, education that stands as clearly practical.

Lutherans, however, draw upon a much richer understanding of the term than either of these understandings. Unlike his sixteenth century contemporaries, Martin Luther spoke of vocation as the call of *all* baptized Christians, not just those entering the monastic life. At the same time, Luther, unlike his twenty-first century descendants, insisted that vocation encompasses *all* of life, not just one's paid occupation. What vocation *is* about, said Luther, is life lived in service to God and to the world. No one Christian is more important than another, whether one is bishop or housewife, priest or baker, king or farmer, parent or child. And no one Christian can live solely to him or herself—all have a call from God to live out their gifts in daily life in service to the neighbor.

If you are a manual laborer, you find that the Bible has been put into your workshop, into your hand, and into your heart. It teaches and preaches how you should treat your neighbor. Just look at your tools—at your needle or thimble, your beer barrel, your goods, your scales or yardsticks or measure—and you will read this statement inscribed on them. Everywhere you look, it stares at you. . . . All this is continually crying out to you: "Friend, use me in your relations with your neighbor just as you would want your neighbor to use his property in his relations with you."[8]

In other words, said Luther, every activity of daily life, no matter how mundane, stands as an opportunity to serve God through serving the neighbor.

In order to live out one's vocation in service to God and neighbor in the most helpful way, Luther believed that one must be well educated. For Luther, education trained both pastors for work in the church and all Christians for their vocations in the world. Education, argued Luther, must be for all, not just for an elite minority. In making his case to civic leaders in 1524, he wrote, "A city's best and greatest welfare, safety, and strength consists . . . in its having many able, learned, wise, honorable, and well-educated citizens."[9] Luther's insistence that *all* children, rich and poor, boys and girls, deserved an education at the behest of the state, fundamentally revolutionized the idea of universal education.

These two emphases—Luther's historic insistence on education as a means of service to the neighbor and to God, coupled with the theological understanding that "education is a human activity through which God blesses individuals and society,"[10]—combined together to lay the groundwork for all future work of the task force.

The Mandate Expands

With this foundation in place, the task force proceeded. However, the foundation itself quickly presented difficulties of its own for the building that would rise upon it. After all, if one took both scripture and Martin Luther's definition of vocation seriously, what truly was *not* encompassed by it? If one accepted that vocation was lived out in every facet of daily life, how could one speak of education in a narrow, focused way? Accepting these understandings soon led members of the task force in a variety of directions, and discussion about what should be included in the social statement began to grow—first by leaps, then by bounds. How could one get a handle on something so amorphous?

In an attempt to begin "harnessing the elephant," the task force brought in a number of presenters with specific expertise in certain areas related to its work. These presentations ranged from panelists who spoke on "Children and Their Development" to "Normative Ethics and the Political Process".[11] The task force even went on field trips to local Lutheran day schools in the Chicago area, meeting with teachers and administrators to discuss the opportunities and challenges such day schools represent.[12]

After hearing from many people throughout the church on a variety of issues, the task force eventually decided that it needed to move beyond the original mandate given to it by the Division for Church in Society. If it was going to take its Lutheran heritage seriously, the task force decided it needed to include discussion and reflection on education in all of its facets—both education as preparation for work in the world (the original charge from the Division) *and* education *in* the faith for the life of the Christian disciple.[13] To educate, the group now explicitly stated, meant also to form in the faith and to encourage discipleship.

Education as Faith Formation

The work of the task force moved into new and unexpected territory. To think about education as also formation in faith raised a new set of questions and issues. Such a definition meant, for example, considering how we shape children, youth, and adults to be disciples and, therefore, by extension, to be evangelists.

One implication of this broadened definition was an understanding that Christian education and faith formation require far more than the simple transmission of knowledge. Indeed, Richard Osmer, Professor of Christian Education at Princeton Theological Seminary, has argued persuasively that to truly educate, to truly form faith in an individual, one must give careful consideration to a teaching style that is holistic and encompasses many elements.

For example, Osmer states that teaching for faith in a holistic way would involve teaching for belief (that is, teaching scripture, traditional doctrines, history and denominational teachings); teaching for relationship (helping individuals connect their beliefs with others in their daily lives); teaching for commitment (helping individuals come to an understanding of and commitment to service to the neighbor); and teaching for mystery (deepening a sense of the sacred and the unanswerable). Each of these four strands proves critical for truly forming children, youth, and adults in the faith.[14]

The need for such a holistic emphasis in forming the faith among Christians today is obvious. Christian Smith, Professor of Sociology at the University of Notre Dame and author of *Soul Searching: The Religious and Spiritual Lives of American Teenagers*, found in his recent research that young people today find it difficult to articulate exactly what they believe in at all. If anything, even *Christian* youth—and often their parents—seem to ascribe more to a "Moral Therapeutic Deism" than they do in the Christian God of tradition and scripture.[15]

Part of what is greatly needed, therefore, is not just improved religious instruction in the church, but even more importantly, an understanding that such education is by its nature holistic and all-encompassing. It goes well beyond creating better church classes and begins primarily with a renewed emphasis on discipleship training in the home. Even Martin Luther recognized this in his own day. When he spoke of educating for the faith, he emphasized the great importance, not just of traditional teachers, but of parents: "Every father of a family is a bishop in his house," Luther proclaimed, "and every wife a bishopess."[16] While the language may sound quaint, it conveys two of Luther's fundamental concepts: that responsibility for training children and youth in the faith is primarily the responsibility of the home, not the church, and that it is a responsibility that falls on both father and mother equally. Both of these affirmations represented new understandings in Luther's day.

At the same time, Luther was a realist. Even in the sixteenth century, he acknowledged that many parents were unprepared for this demanding task and enormous responsibility, either because of unwillingness, incompetence, ignorance, or all three. To aid them in their important duties, Luther wrote *The Small Catechism,* condensing the entire evangelical understanding of the gospel into a book simple enough for a child (and his or her parents) to understand. He also urged pastors, theologians and school teachers to supplement what parents were unable or unwilling to do in the home.

Finally, Luther also emphasized how impossible it was that such learning could end with childhood. Luther noted that even he, biblical professor and initiator of the Protestant Reformation, "must still read and study the Catechism daily, yet I cannot master it as I wish, but must remain a child and pupil of the Catechism, and I do it gladly."[17] To the uninitiated, he wrote, the Catechism seemed "a plain, silly book" most of his scholarly companions disdained. But Luther recognized that, not only did he "read the Catechism," the Catechism "read" him—that in the exchange of reading and study, something fundamental took place to shape the formation of the individual.[18] Here, Luther pointed to the importance of life-long learning—the recognition that individuals never stop learning—or at least, they shouldn't.

Education, Formation, and Evangelism

The task force began to address more seriously the implications of viewing transformative faith formation for vocation as a partnership; a partnership existing not just between home and congregation, but a partnership between home, congregation, and other institutions of the church, such as day schools, preschools, camping and outdoor ministry programs, Lutheran colleges and universities, and campus ministry programs. Each of these, the task force found, contributed to forming faith for vocation in the world and for discipleship. No one individual—whether teacher, parent, or pastor—and no one institution—whether university, preschool, or outdoor ministry—could prove sufficient for the task in and of itself. Each had gifts to offer to the process of education and faith formation, each stood as important in its own right, and each needed to work in partnership with the others in order to truly educate the individual.

Eventually, the task force came to define education in its broadest sense as "learning, teaching, and knowing as a dimension of human life, . . . a lifelong activity that permeates all that we do."[19] This lifelong activity encompasses both education for the world and education for the faith. One's vocation, the task force noted, "begins at baptism and continues throughout life,"[20] and is "a calling from God that encompasses all of life for all the faithful," resulting in a "life lived in joyful response to this call." Therefore, our "calling in education," the task force wrote, is ultimately twofold: while our calling is "to strive with others to ensure that all have access to a high-quality education that develops personal gifts and abilities and serves the common good," it is also a call "to educate people in the Christian faith for their vocation". "This calling," the task force concluded, "embraces all people in both Church and society."[21]

In the course of the work, three main areas covered by the social statement emerged as significant for their implications in the areas of evangelism:

First, building on its understandings of the importance of faith formation, the task force affirmed the importance of the mutuality of the baptismal commitments and promises of parent, sponsors, and church. Such commitments, the task force affirmed, are best lived out in a lifelong partnership involving worship, learning, service, and prayer that leads to a life of formation, discipleship, and service to the neighbor.[22] While the task force did not specifically highlight the implications of this understanding for evangelism, such an understanding of formation and education as vocation and service immediately leads in this direction.

Second, the task force affirmed the profound evangelizing function of certain church-related institutions, including Lutheran preschools and day schools. Because of enormous growth in this area between 1995 and 2006, nearly one in five ELCA congregations now operates some type of Lutheran day school or preschool, schools designed to emphasize, not only academics, but also a "caring Christian environment."[23] This environment, the task force noted, has often not only helped form faith and provide preparation for life in the world for Lutheran children and their families, but has also brought many non-churched parents and their children to membership in the schools' sponsoring congregations.[24] Lutheran schools often stand as more culturally and ethnically diverse than do the congregations sponsoring them and provide significant outreach to their communities. In 2005, for example, at least 17 percent of those attending Lutheran schools were persons of color, "a percentage more than five times higher than ELCA congregations as a whole".[25]

Third, Lutheran involvement in higher education in both Lutheran institutions and in other private and public colleges and universities provides opportunities both to prepare Lutheran students for vocation in the church and world and for outreach to non-Lutheran and non-Christian students. The ELCA itself owns and operates twenty-eight colleges and universities, enrolling nearly fifty-eight thousand students in 2007.[26] Lutheran institutions of higher learning have historically emphasized the liberal-arts tradition and conceived of education in holistic terms, an education that prepares students for work in fields as diverse as law, business, health care, and the arts. By emphasizing critical thinking skills and encouraging students to ask "the essential questions of meaning and purpose," Lutheran institutions of higher education prepare students for the whole of life.[27] Like Lutheran preschools and day schools, Lutheran colleges and universities represent a diverse student population, one often marked by global outreach and cultural and ethnic diversity.[28]

At the same time, Lutheran campus ministries, which operate in public and private non-Lutheran colleges and universities, invite those "in academic settings more deeply into Jesus Christ and the community that bears his name, so that they discover and fulfill their vocation as disciples."[29] Nearly two hundred ELCA-dedicated programs and over four hundred "cooperating congregations" engage in campus ministry across the United States.[30] Campus ministries provide extraordinary opportunities for "both nurturing Lutheran students and reaching out to seekers,"[31] giving them the opportunity "to participate in the life of the Church and deepen their faith during an important time of their lives when they are experiencing change, growth, and challenge."[32]

The Study Guide and Resulting Drafts

In January 2005, the task force published *Our Calling in Education: A Lutheran Study*, a study guide based on its work to that point. Reflecting the expansion of its original mandate, this eighty-two-page study guide proved one of the largest ever produced for an ELCA or predecessor church body. Throughout the church, congregations, individuals, and institutions studied and responded to the document, identifying both strengths and weaknesses.

From October 2005 through early 2006, the task force reviewed all of the responses and formulated a first draft of the social statement itself. The resulting document, *Our Calling in Education: A First Draft of a Social Statement*, became available for comment and study between February and October 2006. Members of the task force led a total of forty-eight hearings in forty synods throughout the ELCA. In addition, the task force received over two hundred responses from individuals and groups who sent in suggestions and critiques of the draft.

In the spring of 2007, based on all of the original research done by the task force and the responses to both the study guide and the first draft, the task force presented its final draft of the proposed social statement, *Our Calling in Education*, to the Division for Church in Society and the ELCA Church Council.[33] The final document contained five major sections plus a prologue and final implementing resolutions for consideration by the August 2007 Churchwide Assembly meeting in Chicago:

- Part I: "What Does God Have to Do with Education?" discussing the Lutheran legacy in education and theological underpinnings of the statement.

- Part II: "What Faith Will Our Children Have?" addressing the responsibility of parents, congregations, and others to form faith in all generations and underpinning the importance of lifelong learning

- Part III: "Will All Children and Youth Have Access to High Quality Education?" expressing both commitment to and expectations of public education as well as discussion of issues of public policy (such as equitable access to quality education, vouchers, educational reforms, and counsel to parents)

- Part IV: "Will Our Church Have Schools and Colleges? Will Our Schools and Colleges Have a Church?" defining the church's commitment to and expectations of Lutheran colleges, universities, and seminaries, Lutheran day schools and centers, and its commitment to lifelong learning.

- Part V: "Will Public Higher Education Serve the Common Good?" outlining the church's commitment to and expectations of public higher education, the role of campus ministry, and issues involved in funding for access to higher education

What Was Learned through This Process?

Taking its heritage seriously and building on Luther's concept of vocation, the final ELCA Social Statement on Education encompassed far more than the framers of the 2001 resolution may have originally intended. Through meetings, hearings, listening posts, forums, and individual responses, the task force heard the voices of thousands of people concerned with the subject of education in the church. The strength of this approach is that Luther's concept of vocation leads one to precisely where this social statement ended up: with a holistic consideration of all of life as education, in all of its facets. The challenge of this approach is to adequately cover in any one document subjects that range from the issue of school vouchers to faith formation in the home.

Along the way, the social statement came to lift up a number of affirmations about what Lutherans have to say on the subject of education.

First, Lutherans have a rich heritage upon which to draw as they think about the concept of education—a concept grounded in Luther's understanding of vocation. Such a model of vocation underlies education in all of its facets, both education in the faith and education for life in the world. A true understanding of vocation necessarily leads one toward discipleship and evangelism.

Second, building on this central understanding of vocation, the resulting social statement posits a *holistic and comprehensive understanding of the concept of education,* one that sees education as connected with both faith and world. Education is far more than "head learning," because it is also forming in the faith for discipleship, a formation that must by its very nature be holistic and experiential, inevitably leading one beyond oneself.

Third, Lutherans support public education. Drawing upon Luther's belief that all children, regardless of social status and background, require and deserve a good education, the statement expresses Lutherans' support for public education. At a time when many people reject the public school system as broken or hopeless, the social statement both affirms and supports public education and calls for accountability in it as well. It calls on congregations, synods, and individual members to partner with public schools in their area to provide mutual support.

Fourth, the resulting social statement is somewhat unique among the social statements produced since the formation of the ELCA in that it addresses *the church and its institutions* as much as its does the church's response to society. Traditionally, social statements have dealt almost exclusively with issues in society and provided guidance to the church and its members as it considers how to respond to these issues and provided direction for the church as it considers issues of public policy.

This social statement, by contrast, stands as much as a teaching document as it does a social statement. While all social statements, to some extent, provide points for theological reflection, this statement does so more than most. *Our Calling in Education* forthrightly addresses the work of the church, not just the life and work of its members in the world. It attempts to call individuals, congregations, and institutions of the church to a reconsideration of some of its most basic principles and asks for a response and rededication to life within our congregations and institutions: to the Lutheran concept of vocation, to the responsibility of parents and children, and to the role of church schools, colleges, and other institutions. The resulting social statement is lengthy because its subject matter is comprehensive, as it deals with both education in the church and the society.

Fifth, although it did not stand as the primary focus of the statement, the study *identified ways in which education often leads to evangelism.* Through its examination of issues as diverse as faith formation in the home to issues related to higher education, the study identified areas where the church is involved in direct outreach to others. Lutheran day schools and ministry in higher education, for example, provide important connections between evangelism and education.

Finally, *social statements rarely provide answers—they stimulate questions.*

The statement provides guidance to the church and attempts to inform conversation and thinking, but it does not attempt to give definitive answers on all issues.[34] The process leading to the social statement results in a living document to be used for continuing discussion, evaluation, and reflection.

The ELCA social statement stands as a case study in definition and in the implications of that definition. In the end, it defined education as "vocation," a vocation lived out in every facet of our lives: from faith formation to discipleship to public schools to higher education. Such education permeates all of life and calls us to be active in all of life. In true education, we are forming faith for work in the world in service to the neighbor. And that work, that service, is finally what evangelism is all about.

Questions for Reflection and Conversation

In your congregations or in personal study, consider the ELCA social statement on education.[35] You may be interested in a particular part of the study (public schools, faith formation in the home, or the use of vouchers, for example), or you may wish to examine the entire document.

1. What new thinking and learning does the social statement spark?

2. What insights can we gain when we consider our lives as vocation?

3. In what ways might the social statement help your congregation rethink its approaches to formation of disciples and evangelists?

4. What public policy issues in your area does the statement address? How might you think differently about these issues after reading the statement?

Parish Strategies

1. The social statement encourages congregations and individuals to develop strong connections to support education. Consider sponsoring a mentoring program with your local public school. What needs does the school have? Tutoring? Reading in classrooms? Teacher support?

2. What educational needs exist in your community? After-school care? Quality Christian day care or day schooling? Consider beginning or partnering with other congregations for ministry in this area.

3. Reach out to a local campus ministry program or church college or university. Consider providing meals, transportation, or their assistance for these important programs.

> *To think about education as formation in faith meant considering how we shape children, youth, and adults to be disciples and, therefore, to be evangelists.*

NOTES

Introduction

1. Letty M. Russell, *Christian Education in Mission* (Philadelphia: Westminster, 1967), 36–37. The "stone" image refers to, "Is there anyone among you who, if your child asks for bread, will give a stone?" (Mt. 7:9). Russell, who for decades has been a divinity school professor, wrote this book in light of her fourteen previous years as a pastor and teacher in the East Harlem Protestant Parish, N.Y.C. She viewed the problems of the inner city not as "an endless source of despair and hopelessness leading to the defeat and retreat of many Protestant churches to the more agreeable middle-class culture of the suburbs," but as a gift, so that people could come to love it, to understand its problems and see it as "an opportunity to participate in Christ's invitation to join in God's mission" (p. 10).

2. Mission Statement of Wartburg Theological Seminary, Dubuque, Iowa, "Wartburg Theological Seminary serves the mission of the Evangelical Lutheran Church in America by being a worship-centered community of critical reflection where learning leads to mission and mission informs learning. Within this community, Wartburg educates women and men to serve the church's mission as ordained and lay leaders. This mission is to proclaim and interpret the gospel of Jesus Christ to a world created for community with God and in need of personal and social healing." http://www.wartburgseminary.edu

3. See chapter 7 "From Learning to Mission to Learning" in Norma Cook Everist, ed., *The Church as Learning Community* (Nashville: Abingdon, 2002), 257–287.

4. *Our Calling in Education: A Lutheran Study,* prepared by the Task Force on Education, Division for church in Society, Evangelical Lutheran Church in America, 2004.

5. *Our Calling in Education: A First Draft of a Social Statement,* prepared by the ELCA Task Force on Education, Church in Society, Evangelical Lutheran Church in America, 2006.

6. Evangelical Lutheran Church in America, "A Vision for Evangelism in the Evangelical Lutheran Church in America," *Evangelical Lutheran Church in America*, 2007, www.elca.org/dcm/evangelism (April 2007).

7. Evangelical Lutheran Church in Canada, "Evangelical Declaration (1997)," *ELCIC*, 2007, http://www.elcic.ca/docs/evandecl.html (April 2007).

8. Telephone interview with Rev. Paul N. Johnson, February 26, 2007.

9. Craig Nessan, "Epilogue: A Lutheran Contribution" in Richard H. Bliese and Craig Van Gelder eds., *The Evangelizing Church* (Minneapolis: Augsburg Fortress, 2005), 133–37.

Chapter 1: Education and Evangelism

1. Other writers in this book would not make such a clear distinction between education and evangelism. See Margaret Krych's chapter 2 as one example.

2. Darrell L. Gruder, *The Continuing Conversion of the Church* (Grand Rapids: Eerdmans, 2000), 23.

3. Richard H. Bliese and Craig Van Gelder, eds., *The Evangelizing Church: A Lutheran Contribution* (Minneapolis: Augsburg Fortress, 2005).

4. Bliese and Van Gelder, 9, 45–47.

5. See Doug Pagitt, *Church Re-Imagined: The Spiritual Formation of People in Communities of Faith and the Solomon's Porch Community* (Grand Rapids: Zondervan, 2005), 19–20.

6. Doug Pagitt, 19–20.

7. The ELCA, along with other Christian churches, has taken a clear stand in support of public schools and the necessity to provide quality education for all children and youth. See chapter 8 in this book for a discussion of the ELCA's position.

8. See Robert Richard Osmer, *The Teaching Ministry of Congregations* (Louisville: Westminster John Knox, 2005), 27.

9. Horace Bushnell, *Christian Nurture* (Grand Rapids: Baker Book House), 10.

10. Paul J. Achtemeier, ed., *Harper's Bible Dictionary* (San Francisco: Harper and Row Publishers, 1985), s.v. "Disciple".

11. John Westerhoff is a Christian educator who has, in many ways, supported this point of view. One of the many places he discusses the primary role that the faith community plays in the educational process is his book *Will Our Children Have Faith?* (New York: Seabury, 1976). On the other hand, Norma Cook Everist, one of the writers in this book, lifts up the church as a learning community, but also stresses the need for intentionality in relation to Christian education. See her book *The Church as Learning Community* (Nashville: Abingdon, 2002).

12. My definition of "understanding" has been greatly influenced by Grant Wiggins and Jay McTighe in *Understanding by Design*, 2nd ed. (Alexandria, VA.: Association for Supervision and Curriculum Development, 2005). See especially chapter 2, "Understanding Understanding," and chapter 4, "The Six Facets of Understanding."

13. From email correspondence with Erick Nelson, a layperson who has a strong interest in what it means to love God with our minds.

14. From email correspondence with Erick Nelson.

15. The notion of conversion as a form of relearning is from Diana Butler Bass's book *Christianity for the Rest of Us: How the Neighborhood Church Is Transforming the Faith* (San Francisco: HarperSanFrancisco, 2006), 65 and 274.

16. Mary Hess discusses this understanding of education in relation to teaching in chapter 9 of this book when she explores Parker Palmer's "community of truth".

17. Sara Little, *To Set One's Heart: Belief and Teaching in the Church* (Atlanta: John Knox Press, 1983), 5.

18. Little, 16. Italics in original.

19. Little, 17. Italics in original.

20. Little, 7.

21. Craig Dykstra and Dorothy C. Bass, "Times of Yearning, Practices of Faith," in *Practicing Our Faith: A Way of Life for a Searching People*, ed. Dorothy C. Bass (San Francisco: Jossey-Bass, 1997), 5. For a brief discussion of other ways of defining "practice", see Craig Dykstra and Dorothy C. Bass "A Theological Understanding of Christian Practices," in *Practicing Theology: Beliefs and Practices in Christian Life*, ed. Miroslav Volf and Dorothy C. Bass (Grand Rapids: William B. Eerdmans Publishing Company, 2002), 20.

22. This list is taken from Dorothy C. Bass, *Practicing Our Faith*, and Diana Butler Bass, *Christianity for the Rest of Us*. It does not include all of the practices identified in either of these volumes. Another list of practices can be found in *Growing in the Life of Faith: Education in Christian Practices* by Craig Dykstra (Louisville: Geneva, 1999), 42.

23. Amy Plantinga Pauw, "Attending to the Gaps between Beliefs and Practices," in Volf and Bass, *Practicing Theology,* ed. Volf and Bass, 36.

24. Bass, *Christianity for the Rest of Us*, 198.

25. Kieran Egan, *Imagination in Teaching and Learning* (Chicago: University of Chicago Press, 1992), 43.

Chapter 2: What Are the Theological Foundations?

1. Martin Luther's Preface to the Small Catechism, *The Book of Concord*, ed. Robert Kolb and Timothy Wengert (Minneapolis: Fortress Press, 2000), 347.

2. For Tillich on Question and Answer and correlation, see the Introduction to Paul Tillich, *Systematic Theology* (Chicago: University of Chicago Press, 1951) 3–68 and especially 1:18–28.

3. Paul Tillich, *Systematic Theology*, 3 vols. (Chicago: University of Chicago Press, 1951, 1957, and 1963).

4. Paul Tillich, *Theology of Culture* (New York: Oxford University Press, 1964), 206.

5. Martin Luther, *The Book of Concord*, ed. Robert Kolb and Timothy J. Wengert (Minneapolis: Fortress Press, 2000), 380.

6. Luther, 381.

7. Tillich, *Systematic Theology* (Chicago: University of Chicago Press, 1963), 3:193.

8. Tillich, 3:193.

9. Tillich, 3:193.

10. Tillich, 3:194.

11. Tillich, 3:194.

12. Tillich, 3:104.

13. Tillich, 3:194

14. See Martin Luther, "To the Councilmen of all Cities in Germany That They Establish and Maintain Christian Schools" in *Luther's Works* (Philadelpia: Fortress Press, 1962) 45:339–78.

15. Martin Luther, "A Sermon on Keeping Children in School", in *Luther's Works* (Philadelphia, Fortress Press, 1967), 46:207–258.

16. Tillich, 3:194

17. Tillich, 3:195.

18. Tillich, 3:195.

19. Tillich, 3:196

20. See Tillich, *Theology of Culture*, 154–5.

21. See Tillich, 3:185–7.

22. See Tillich, *Theology of Culture*, 202–3.

23. Tillich, *Systematic Theology* 3:74, 211–3, 260–1.

24. Tillich, *Systematic Theology* 1:240–241 and 3:253–255. And, Paul Tillich, *Dynamics of Faith* (New York: Harper and Row, 1957), cha. 3.

25. See Margaret A. Krych, *Teaching the Gospel Today* (Minneapolis: Augsburg, 1987), 52–3.

26. Gerhard Ebeling, *God and Word*, trans. James W. Leitch (Philadelphia: Fortress Press, 1967), 34–49.

27. See Dietrich Bonhoeffer, *Letters and Papers from Prison* (London: SCM Press, 1959), 109, 118, 122.

28. Wolfhart Pannenberg, *Systematic Theology* III (Grand Rapids, MI: William B. Eerdmans, 1993), 391.

29. Richard H. Bliese, "Addressing Captives in Babylon" in *The Evangelizing Church: A Lutheran Contribution*, Richard H. Bliese and Craig Van Gelder, ed., (Minneapolis: Augsburg Fortress, 2005), 39.

30. Pannenberg, *Systematic Theology*, 3:46.

31. "In Christ they already receive justification and pardon at the hands of the future Judge." Ibid., 616.

32. See Paul Tillich, "Creative Love in Education" in *World Christian Education*, 18:3.

Chapter 3: How Do We Maket the Gospel Come Alive?

1. Kent S. Knutson, "A New Look At Evangelism," Address to the Sixth General Convention of the American Lutheran Church, in *1972 Reports and Actions*, ed. A.R. Mickelson, Exhibit F-4, 1,139.

2. "Holy Baptism" in *Evangelical Lutheran Worship* (Minneapolis: Augsburg Fortress, 2006), 231.

3. Knutson, 1, 138.

4. Martin Luther, "The Magnificat" in *Luther's Works*, ed. J. Pelikan (St. Louis: Concordia Publishing House, 1956), 21:299.

5. For a provocative and insightful discussion of the limits of thinking of the gospel as "story," see Richard Lischer, "The Limits of Story" in *Interpretation* 38:01, pp 26 ff, in which Lischer identifies four limits to the usefulness of understanding the

gospel as story. To think of the gospel as primarily story, he argues, restricts us because it overlays a preconceived storylike pattern onto the biblical witness. He notes that this shape "does not always reflect the way things are but mercifully—or arrogantly—imposes a pattern on the disorder and anarchy of life as it is. . . . The stories we tell may provide the sense of order so desperately needed *or* they may appear transparently palliative to those whose experience has resisted the broom that sweeps in one direction" (30).

6. Robert F. Taft, S. J., *Beyond East and West: Problems in Liturgical Understanding,* 2nd ed. (Rome: Pontifical Oriental Institute, 2001), 23.

7. Romans 1:16 ff.

8. Martin Luther, "The Babylonian Captivity of the Church" in *Luther's Works,* ed. H. T. Lehmann (Philadelphia: Fortress Press, 1959), 36:42.

9. See Dan Erlander, *Manna and Mercy: A Brief History of God's Unfolding Promise to Mend the Entire Universe* (Minneapolis: Augsburg/Fortress Press, 1992).

10. 2 Corinthians 5:18-19.

11. Mark 12:30.

12. Parker J. Palmer, *The Courage to Teach: Exploring The Inner Landscape of a Teacher's Life* (San Francisco: Jossey-Bass, 1998), 105.

13. Parker J. Palmer, *To Know as We Are Known: Education as a Spiritual Journey* (San Francisco: HarperSanFrancisco, 1983), 31.

14. Robert F. Taft, S. J., *Beyond East and West: Problems in Liturgical Understanding,* 2nd ed. (Rome: Pontifical Oriental Institute, 2001), 28.

15. Kathleen Norris, *Amazing Grace: A Vocabulary of Faith* (New York: Riverhead Books, 1998), 303.

16. "Post Communion Prayer" in *Evangelical Lutheran Worship,* 74.

17. Robert Lowry, "How Can I Keep From Singing?" in *With One Voice: A Lutheran Resource for Worship* (Minneapolis: Augsburg Fortress, 1995), hymn 781.

18. Martin Luther, "The Freedom of a Christian" in *Luther's Works,* ed. H. T. Lehmann (Philadelphia: Fortress Press, 1957), 31:371.

Chapter 4: How Do We Move from Apathy?

1. Leslie Newbigin, *The Gospel in a Pluralistic Society* (Grand Rapids: W. B. Erdmanns, 1989), 244.

2. Craig L. Nessan, "After the Death of Evangelism" in *The Evangelizing Church: A Lutheran Contribution,* ed. Richard H. Bliese and Craig Van Gelder (Minneapolis: Augsburg Fortress, 2005), 114.

3. Kelly Fryer, "The Gift is a Call" in *The Evangelizing Church: A Lutheran Contribution,* ed. Richard H. Bliese and Craig Van Gelder (Minneapolis: Augsburg Fortress, 2005), 28.

4. Carl E. Braaten, "Preaching Christ in an Age of Religious Pluralism" in *Word and World* 9/3 (Summer 1989), 249

5. Emil Brunner, *The Word and the World* (New York: Charles Scribner's Sons, 1931), 108.

6. Brunner, 108.

7. Nessan, "After the Death of Evangelism," 114.

Chapter 7: Reaching Out

1. Jon Diefenthaler, "Lutheran Schools in America" in *Religious Schooling in America*, ed. James C. Carper and Thomas C. Hunt, (Birmingham: Religious Education Press, 1984).

2. See "The Small Catechism" in *The Book of Concord: Luther's Works*, vols. 45 and 46.

3. Lawrence Cremin, *American Education: The National Experience* (New York: Harper Torch Books, 1988), ix.

4. Richard H. Bliese and Craig Van Gelder, eds., *The Evangelizing Church: A Lutheran Contribution* (Minneapolis: Augsburg Fortress, 2005), 9.

5. Correspondence from Braband to Strobert, February 17, 2006.

6. R. Kolb, *The Book of Concord: The Confessions of the Evangelical Lutheran Church* (Minneapolis: Fortress Press, 2000), 319.

7. Nelson T. Strobert, "Pastoral Educational Leadership Preparation and Schools" in *Views and Vision* 6 (Spring 2005) 4-5.

8. Melvin M. Kieschnick. *The Pastor and the Lutheran School* (Itasca, IL: Wheat Ridge Ministries, 1987, rev. ed. 2002), 13-33.

9. Gallup, September 2006.

10. It should be noted that ELCA Lutheran schools and early childhood centers reflect the racial and ethnic diversity of their surrounding communities. See Department for Research and Evaluation, ELCA. "Summary: ELCA Schools and ECE Centers Survey 2003–2004," February 2004, 4.

11. Barna Update, March 14, 2005.

12. John Westerhoff, *Will Our Children Have Faith*, rev. ed. (Harrisburg, PA: Morehouse Press, 1999), 128.

Chapter 8: Abiding in the Word

1. Kelly Fryer, "The Gift Is a Call" in *The Evangelizing Church: A Lutheran Contribution,* ed. Richard H. Bliese and Craig Van Gelder (Minneapolis: Augsburg Fortress, 2005), 12.

2. R. W. Burtner and R. E. Chiles, *A Compend of Wesley's Theology* (New York: Abingdon, 1954), 261. In a letter to James Hervey, John Wesley wrote, *"I look upon all the world as my parish."*

3. See chapter 11 in this book.

4. Carol Gilligan, *In a Different Voice: Psychological Theory and Women's Development* (Cambridge: Harvard University Press, 1982).

5. See James Dittes, *Men at Work: Life Beyond the Office* (Louisville: Westminster John Knox, 1996) and *Driven by Hope: Men and Meaning* (Louisville: Westminster John Knox, 1996).

6. National Congregations Study (NCS) of 1998, as quoted in David Murrow's *Why Men Hate Going to Church* (Nashville: Thomas Nelson, Inc., 2005), 54–55.

7. Murrow, 29–30.

8. Murrow, 224.

9. Murrow, 92–94.

10. Murrow, 175–76.

11. David W. Anderson, Paul G. Hill, and Roland D. Martinson, Coming of Age: Exploring the Identity and Spirituality of Younger Men (Minneapolis Augsburg Fortress, 2006), 54

12. Murrow, 59.

13. Murrow, 72.

14. Murrow, 180.

15. Murrow, 136.

16. Murrow, 207–14.

17. Murrow, 200–15.

18. An example is *Beginnings: An Introduction to Christian Faith,* written by Andy Langford and Mark Ralls, video resources by Rob Weber (Nashville: Abingdon Press, 2003). This material focuses each week on a question like, "Why am I not where I want to be?" (on sin and the cross), "Can I start again?" (on forgiveness and wholeness), and "Why should I join any group that will have me as a member ?" (on the nature of the church).

19. "Americans and the God Question" *The Christian Science Monitor,* September 25, 2006, http://csmonitor.com. (May 2007)

20. "Losing My Religion? No, Says Baylor Religion Survey," Baylor University Public Relations News, September 11, 2006.

21. Hannah Elliott, "Americans Believe in Four Gods, Baylor Religion Study Finds," *ChurchExecutive.com (n.d.),* http://www.ChurchExecutive.com. (May 2007).

22. Anne Neufeld Ruff, *Growing Together: Understanding and Nurturing Your Child's Faith Journey* (Newton, Kansas: Faith and Life Press, 1996), 26–27.

23. Ruff, 27–28

24. Ruff, 27–28.

Chapter 9: Go and Make Learners!

1. Robert Kegan and Lisa Lahey, *How the Way We Talk Can Change the Way We Work* (San Francisco: Jossey-Bass, 2002).

2. This, of course, is also part of the energy behind the research methodology known as "apppreciative inquiry." See David Cooperrider, Frank Barrett, Suresh Srivastva,

"Social Construction and Appreciative Inquiry: A Journey in Organizational Theory," in *Management and Organization: Relational Alternatives to Individualism*, ed. D. M. Hosking, H. P. Dachler and K. J. Gergen (New York: Ashgate Publishing, 1995). Also, Mark Lau Branson, *Memories, Hopes and Conversations: Appreciative Inquiry and Congregational Change* (Herndon, VA: Alban Institute, 2004).

3. Indeed, I fear that one of the side effects, or "incidental" learnings, that many people might take from the recent—and quite powerful—book, *The Evangelizing Church: A Lutheran Contribution* (Augsburg, 2005) eds. by Richard Bliese and Craig Van Gelder —is that in an effort to highlight the urgent need to move into evangelization, the authors might at the same time be inadvertently perpetuating a painful stereotype (that is, Lutherans are not evangelizers) that relies on negative assertions to make its point.

4. See Parker Palmer, *The Courage to Teach* (San Francisco: Jossey-Bass, 1997) and *To Know as We Are Known* (San Francisco: Harper & Row, 1993).

5. The "null curriculum" is that which is not taught, but which also has consequences.

6. Palmer, *The Courage to Teach*, 106 ff.

7. Palmer's critique and proposal are most clearly elaborated in *To Know as We Are Known* and *The Courage to Teach*.

8. I Cor 2:1-5 NAB.

9. Kegan and Lahey, *How the Way We Talk Can Change the Way We Work*,102.

10. It is worth noting that Sharon Daloz Park's work on leadership education suggests that "it must be underscored that it is the reflection on one's own experiences of leadership failure that is the essential, vital feature of this leadership formation practice." Sharon Daloz Parks, *Leadership Can Be Taught: A Bold Approach for a Complex World* (Boston: Harvard Business School Publishing Corporation, 2005), 96.

11. See Stephen Brookfield, *Becoming a Critically Reflective Teacher* (San Francisco: Jossey-Bass, 1995), particularly chapter six.

12. Craig Van Gelder, "For the Sake of the World" in *The Evangelizing Church: A Lutheran Contribution*, ed. Richard Bliese and Craig Van Gelder (Minneapolis: Augsburg Fortress, 2005), 67.

13. Jack Fortin's eloquent, short book *Centered Life* (Minneapolis: Augsburg Fortress, 2005) is an excellent example of how to do this.

14. Kegan and Lahey, *How the Way We Talk Can Change the Way We Work*,114.

15. Kegan and Lahey, 128–29.

16. Kegan and Lahey, 141.

17. Mark Edwards names a series of Christian virtues in relation to this kind of humility as being quintessential scholarly responses in his essay, "Characteristically Lutheran Leanings?" in *Dialog: A Journal of Theology*, vol. 41, #1, Spring 2002.

18. Kegan and Lahey, *How the Way We Talk Can Change the Way We Work*, 143-145.

19. Palmer, *To Know as We Are Known,* 43.

Chapter 10: Go and Listen

1. Warren Clark and Grant Schellenberg "Who's Religious?" *Statistics Canada,* 2006, http://www.statsCanada.ca/English/freepub/11/008/XIE/200600/Main_religious. htm. (May 2007).

2. Jeremy Langford, *God Moments: Why Faith Really Matters to a New Generation* (Maryknoll, NY.: Orbis Books, 2001).

3. Langford, 14.

4. Sharon Daloz Parks, *Big Questions, Worthy Dreams: Mentoring Young Adults in Their Search for Meaning, Purpose and Faith* (San Francisco: Jossey-Bass, 2000).

5. Tom Beaudoin, *Virtual Faith: The Irreverent Spiritual Quest of Generation X* (San Francisco: Jossey-Bass, 1998), 13.

6. Francis Bridger, "Desperately Seeking What? Engaging With the New Spiritual Quest," *Journal of Christian Education,* vol. 44. no. 1 (2001), 10.

7. Bridger, 11.

8. Tom Beaudoin, *Virtual Faith: The Irreverent Spiritual Quest of Generation X* (San Francisco: Jossey-Bass, 1998), 45.

9. Douglas Rushkoff, "Media: It's the Real Thing," *New Perspectives Quarterly,* 11 (3) (1994), 8.

10. See Mary E. Hess, *Engaging Technology in Theological Education: All That We Can't Leave Behind* (Lanham, MD: Rowman & Litchfield, 2005).

Chapter 11: Learn to Share Christ

1. Suzanne de Dietrich, *The Witnessing Community* (Philadelphia: The Westminster Press, 1958), 16–17. De Dietrich wrote that the Church's vocation is as the witnessing community taken out of the world, set apart for God, but set apart in order to be again sent to the world. Separation and mission are both necessary. Two temptations, therefore, are either considering the separate life an end in itself or succumbing to a slow process of assimilation by which God's people lose their identity.

2. Letty M. Russell, *Human Liberation in a Feminist Perspective: A Theology* (Philadelphia: Westminster: 1974), 53.

3. Norma Cook Everist and Craig L. Nessan, eds., *Forming an Evangelizing People* (Dubuque: Wartburg Theological Seminary, 2005), 20.

Chapter 12: Rededicate Ourselves

1. "Guiding Perspectives for Social Statements" in *Policies and Procedures of the ELCA for Addressing Social Concerns,* (1998), 10–13, available at *Evangelical Church In America,* 2007, http://www.elca.org/socialstatements/procedures/perspectives.html (May 2007).

2. *A Call for a Social Statement on Education,* Action taken by the Churchwide Assembly, meeting in Indianapolis, Indiana, August 8-14, 2001.

3. From action of the Board of the Division for Church in Society, October 2002, in *Our Calling in Education: A Lutheran Study* (Chicago: Task Force on Education, Division for Church in Society, Evangelical Lutheran Church in America, 2004), 3.

4. At its second meeting in January 2004, the task force received papers and participated in a panel discussion with Rolf Jacobson on "Biblical Perspectives on Education," Marilyn Harran on "Reflections on Martin Luther and Childhood Education," Harran, "Martin Luther and Education: Ideas for the Twenty-First Century" and Darrell Jodock on "The Lutheran Tradition and Education." All of the papers are available at the Web site for the ELCA Social Statement at http://www.elca.org/socialstatements/education/studyhtml.

5. *Our Calling in Education: A Lutheran Study*, 18.

6. *Our Calling in Education: A Lutheran Study*, 20.

7. *Our Calling in Education: A Lutheran Study*, 20.

8. Martin Luther, *Luther's Works*, ed. Jaroslav Pelikan (St. Louis: Concordia, 1956), 21:237.

9. Martin Luther, To the Councilmen of All Cities in Germany that They Establish and Maintain Christian Schools (1524) *Luther's Works*, ed. Walther I. Brandt (Philadelphia: Muhlenberg Press, 1962), 45:356.

10. *Our Calling in Education: A Lutheran Study*, 18.

11. Additional papers presented to the task force during the course of its work included the following: Robert Benne, "Lutheran Quietism in Higher Education?"; Jerome Berryman, "Children and Mature Spirituality;" Denise Shiver, "Faith and Education: Some Thoughts;" Don Strickland, "Normative Ethics and the Political Process;" Emily Van Dunk, "A Sample of Issues in K-12 Education;" Beth Venzke, "Educating ALL Children" and Grace Wolf-Chase, "The ELCA Social Statement—Some Comments." The following papers presented to the task force are also available online at www.elca.org/socialstatements/education/studyhtml.html. Robert Benne, "If I Had It to Do Over Again;" Marcia Bunge, "Rediscovering the Dignity and Complexity of Children: Resources from the Christian Tradition;" Paul Dovre, "The Vocation of a Lutheran Liberal Arts College Revisited;" Christi Lines, "Reflections of a Lutheran Elementary School Principal;" Leonard Schulze, "Vocation: The Crux of the Matter;" Emily Van Dunk, "School Choice in Milwaukee," Grace Wolf-Chase, "Reflections on Creation," and Jean Ziettlow, "The Stages of Faith Development."

12. The task force visited Bethel Christian School in West Garfield and Bethel New Life in Chicago during its January 2004 meeting. For additional discussion on the role of Lutheran schools in evangelism, the chapter 7 in this volume by Nelson Strobert.

13. In reality, the original mandate from the Board of the Division for Church in Society pointed in this direction from the beginning—although it may not have realized it. By asking the social statement to deal with both church and world—asking it to consider for example, the role of Lutheran schools as well as issues involving public schools it opened the door for consideration of education in its many facets.

14. Richard Osmer, *Teaching for Faith: A Guide for Teachers of Adult Classes* (Louisville: Westminster John Knox, 1992), 13–28.

15. Christian Smith, *Soul Searching: The Religious and Spiritual Lives of American Teenagers* (New York: Oxford University Press, 2005), in particular, 136, 162 ff., and 262.

16. Martin Luther, *Ten Sermons on the Catechism* (1528) from the Introduction to the First Commandment in *Luther's Works*, ed. and trans. John W. Doberstein (Philadelphia: Fortress Press, 1959), 51:137.

17. Martin Luther, "Preface to the *Large Catechism*" in *The Book of Concord: The Confessions of the Evangelical Lutheran Church*, ed. Robert Kolb and Timothy J. Wengert, (Minneapolis: Fortress Press, 2000), 380.

18. Muendel, H. Dittmar, "Educating the Heart: Christian Nurture," *Consensus: A Canadian Lutheran Journal of Theology*, 11:3, July 1985, 3–12.

19. *Our Calling in Education: Proposed Social Statement* (Chicago: Task Force on Education, Division for Church in Society, Evangelical Lutheran Church in America, 2007), 4.

20. *Our Calling*, 12.

21. *Our Calling*, 2.

22. *Our Calling*, 3, 13, 21.

23. *Our Calling*, 34.

24. For more on Lutheran schools and evangelism, see chapter 7 in this book by Nelson Strobert. In 2006 ELCA congregations owned and operated 267 elementary schools, 18 high schools, and 1,722 early childhood centers, involving more than 225,000 students. (Statistics for 2005–06 school year provided by Donna Braband, director for Schools and Early Childhood Centers, Vocation and Education). For more information on ELCA centers and schools see the Web page of the ELCA Schools and Early Childhood Ministries of the Vocation and Education unit (*www.elca.org/schools*).

25. *Our Calling*, 35.

26. Information on ELCA colleges and universities is found on the Web page of ELCA Colleges and Universities of the Vocation and Education unit (www.elca.org/colleges). At the beginning of the 2006-2007 school year, there were 50,088 full-time undergraduate students, 2,271 full-time graduate students, 3,892 part-time undergraduate students, 1,670 part-time graduate students, for a total of 57,921 students, which includes 55,224 full-time students in ELCA colleges and universities. Figures provided by Dr. Arne Selbyg, director for Colleges and Universities, Vocation and Education Unit of the ELCA.

27. *Our Calling*, 37.

28. *Our Calling*, 38.

29. "Policies and Procedures for Campus Ministries," approved by the ELCA Church Council (November 15, 2003), 4 (www.elca.org/campusministry/policies), from *Proposed Social Statement*, 46.

30. For more information visit the Web site of ELCA Lutheran Campus Ministry in the Vocation and Education unit (www.elca.org/campusministry).

31. *Proposed Social Statement*, 46.

32. *Proposed Social Statement*, 45.

33. The text of the final document is available at www.elca.org/socialstatements/education.

34. Robert D. Haak, *Intersections*, Summer 2006, 4.

35. The statement is available online at www.elca.org/campusministry.

BIBLIOGRAPHY

Bass, Diana Butler. *Christianity for the Rest of Us: How the Neighborhood Church Is Transforming the Faith.* San Francisco: HarperSanFrancisco, 2006.

Beaudoin, Tom. *Virtual Faith: The Irreverent Spiritual Quest of Generation X.* San Francisco: Jossey-Bass, 1998.

Billing, Einar. *Our Calling.* Minneapolis: Fortress Press, 1964.

Bliese, Richard H., and Craig Van Gelder, ed. *The Evangelizing Church: A Lutheran Contribution.* Minneapolis: Augsburg Fortress, 2005.

Bonhoeffer, Dietrich. *Life Together.* New York: Harper & Row, 1954.

Branson, Mark Lau. *Memories, Hopes and Conversations: Appreciative Inquiry and Congregational Change.* Herndon, VA: Alban Institute, 2004.

Brookfield, Stephen. *Becoming a Critically Reflective Teacher.* San Francisco: Jossey-Bass, 1995.

Bushnell, Horace. *Christian Nurture.* Grand Rapids: Baker Book House, 2007.

Carper, James C., and Thomas C. Hunt, eds. *Religious Schooling in America.* Birmingham, AL: Religious Education Press, 1984.

Confirmation: Engaging Lutheran Foundations and Practice, Foreword by Margaret A. Krych. Minneapolis: Augsburg Fortress, 1999.

de Dietrich, Suzanne. *The Witnessing Community.* Philadelphia: The Westminster Press, 1958.

Diehl, William E. *The Monday Connection.* San Francisco: HarperSanFrancisco, 1991.

Dittes, James. *Driven by Hope: Men and Meaning.* Louisville: Westminster John Knox, 1996.

Dykstra, Craig. *Growing in the Life of Faith: Education in Christian Practices.* Louisville: Geneva Press, 1999.

Dykstra, Craig, and Dorothy C. Bass. *Practicing Our Faith: A Way of Life for a Searching People.* San Francisco: Jossey-Bass, 1997.

Egan, Kieran. *Imagination in Teaching and Learning.* Chicago: The University of Chicago Press, 1992.

Erlander, Dan. *Manna and Mercy: A Brief History of God's Unfolding Promise to Mend the Entire Universe.* Minneapolis: Augsburg/Fortress Press, 1995.

Everist, Norma Cook. *The Church As Learning Community.* Nashville: Abingdon Press, 2002.

Fortin, Jack. *Centered Life.* Minneapolis: Augsburg Fortress, 2005.

Gilligan, Carol. *In a Different Voice: Psychological Theory and Women's Development.* Cambridge, Mass.: Harvard University Press, 1982.

Grothe, Rebecca, ed. *Lifelong Learning.* Minneapolis: Augsburg Fotress, 1997.

Gruder, Darrell L. *The Continuing Conversion of the Church.* Grand Rapids: Eerdmans, 2000.

Hess, Mary E. *Engaging Technology in Theological Education: All that We Can't Leave Behind.* Lanham, MD: Rowman & Litchfield, 2005.

Hunter, George G. *The Celtic Way of Evangelism: How Christianity Can Reach the West— Again.* Nashville: Abingdon, 2000.

Kegan, Robert, and Lisa Lahey. *How the Way We Talk Can Change the Way We Work.* San Francisco: Jossey-Bass, 2002.

Kieschnick, Melvin M. *The Pastor and the Lutheran School.* Itasca, IL: Wheat Ridge Ministries, 1987, rev. ed. 2002.

Krych, Margaret A. *Teaching the Gospel Today.* Minneapolis: Augsburg, 1987.

Langford, Jeremy. *God Moments: Why Faith Really Matters to a New Generation.* Maryknoll, NY: Orbis Books, 2001.

Little, Sara, *To Set One's Heart: Belief and Teaching in the Church.* Atlanta: John Knox, 1983.

Luther, Martin. "The Freedom of a Christian" in *Luther's Works.* Vol. 31. Ed. H. T. Lehmann. Philadelphia: Fortress Press, 1957.

———. "A Sermon on Keeping Children in School" in *Luther's Works.* Vol. 46. Ed. H. T. Lehmann. Philadelphia: Fortress Press, 1957.

———. *Ten Sermons on the Catechism* (1528) from the Introduction to the First Commandment in *Luther's Works.* Vol. 51. Ed. and trans. John W. Doberstein. Philadelphia: Fortress Press, 1959.

———. *To the Councilmen of All Cities in Germany that They Establish and Maintain Christian Schools* (1524) in *Luther's Works.* Vol. 45. Ed. Walther I. Brandt. Philadelphia: Muhlenberg Press, 1962.

The Ministry of Children's Education, with an introduction by Krych, Margaret A., Krych. Minneapolis: Augsburg Fortress, 2004.

Murrow, David. *Why Men Hate Going to Church.* Nashville: Thomas Nelson, Inc., 2005.

Nessan, Craig L. *Beyond Maintenance to Mission: A Theology of the Congregation.* Minneapolis: Fortress Press, 1999.

Neufeld, Anne. *Growing Together: Understanding and Nurturing Your Child's Faith Journey.* Newton, Kansas: Faith and Life Press, 1996.

Newbigin, Leslie. *The Gospel in a Pluralistic Society.* Grand Rapids, MI: W. B. Erdmanns, 1989.

Pagitt, Doug. *Church Re-Imagined: The Spiritual Formation of People in Communities of Faith and the Solomon's Porch Community.* Grand Rapids: Zondervan, 2005.

Palmer, Parker J. *The Courage to Teach: Exploring the Inner Landscape of a Teacher's Life.* San Francisco: Jossey-Bass Publishers, 1998.

———. *To Know as We Are Known: Education as a Spiritual Journey.* San Francisco: HarperSanFrancisco, 1983.

Parks, Sharon Daloz. *Big Questions, Worthy Dreams: Mentoring Young Adults in Their Search for Meaning, Purpose and Faith.* San Francisco: Jossey-Bass, 2000.

Roloff, Marvin L., ed. *Education for Christian Living.* Minneapolis: Augsburg Fortress, 1987.

Russell, Letty M. *Christian Education in Mission.* Philadelphia: Westminster: 1967.

Schreiter, Robert J. *The Ministry of Reconciliation: Spirituality and Strategies.* Markyknoll, NY: Orbis, 1998.

Seymour, Jack L., Margaret Ann Crain, and Joseph V. Crockett. *Educating Christians: The Intersection of Meaning, Learning, and Vocation.* Nashville: Abingdon, 1993.

Strobert, Nelson T. "Pastoral Educational Leadership Preparation and Schools," *Views and Vision* 6: Spring 2005.

Task Force on Education. *Our Calling in Education: Proposed Social Statement.* Chicago: Division for Church in Society, Evangelical Lutheran Church in America, 2007.

Thomsen, Mark W. *Christ Crucified: A 21st Century Missiology of the Cross.* Minneapolis: Lutheran University Press, 2004.

Tillich, Paul. *Dynamics of Faith.* New York: Harper and Row, 1957.

———. *Theology of Culture.* New York: Oxford University Press, 1964.

Westerhoff, John. *Will Our Children Have Faith?* New York: Seabury, 1976.

Wiggins, Grant, and Jay McTighe. *Understanding by Design.* 2nd ed. Alexandria, VA: Association for Supervision and Curriculum Development, 2005.

INDEX

Acts
    Acts 1:8, 45
    Acts 2:1-11, 88, 128
    Acts 2:37-42, 77
    Acts 4:1-4, 77
    Acts 4:20, 122
    Acts 8:26-39, 88, 93
    Acts 9:2, xii
    Acts 15, 67
    Acts 18:24-25, 92

Adults, 55–56, 102, 103
    Adult education, viii, 2, 3, 12, 24, 57, 60, 84, 106, 107, 108, 130
    Unchurched adults, 23, 28, 29
    Adults with developmental disabilities, 59–60
    Older adults, 119

Baptism, 22, 23, 25, 27, 32, 94
Bible Study, 5, 25, 28, 39, 48, 56, 57, 60, 61, 64, 66, 71, 76, 89–91, 95, 129, 137
Biblical literacy, 12
Body of Christ, xi, 27, 34, 127
Bonhoeffer, Dietrich, 31

Catechism, 22, 25, 47, 76, 140
Children 12, 13, 19, 27, 28, 29, 54–56, 59–61, 96, 102, 104, 138–144
Collaboration, 68, 108, 131
Community
    Asian community, 65
    Christian community, xi, 1, 11, 25, 32, 34, 101, 127
    Community outreach, 62, 78
    Faith community, 13, 14, 15, 19, 20, 32, 38, 53, 56, 78, 79, 81, 126, 127, 130, 132
    Global community, 3, 66, 70

    Koinania, 70
    Spiritual community, 27
Confirmation, 60, 61, 75
Corinthians
    1 Cor. 1:18, 45
    1 Cor. 1:25, 45
    1 Cor. 8, 67
    1 Cor. 5:18–19, 105
    1 Cor. 13:12–13, 16
Creed, 22, 66, 125, 126, 128
    Apostle's Creed, 46, 126
Culture
    Culture and education, 12, 20, 28, 29, 107, 123
    Culture and evangelism, 26
    Culture and worship, 19
    Culture of congregation, 70–71
    Multicultural, 59, 65, 66, 67, 68, 71, 72, 73, 74, 130
    Popular culture and youth, 115–117, 118–119, 119–120
Cyberspace, 5, 118–121

Disciples/discipleship, xi, xii, 2, 3, 4, 6, 11, 12, 13, 14, 17, 19, 20, 23, 25, 40, 43, 47, 57, 58, 59, 60, 61, 67, 77, 79, 85, 88, 92, 95, 96, 101, 109, 123, 126, 127, 128, 129, 131, 132, 134, 140, 141, 142, 143, 144

ELCA (Evangelical Lutheran Church in America), 1, 2, 3, 76, 78, 79, 82, 102, 124, 135–136, 141–143
ELCIC (Evangelical Lutheran Church in Canada), 1, 2, 3

Gender, 88, 90
    Men, 90–92, 95, 112, 129, 131
    Men and Women, 5, 39, 41, 88, 92, 96
    Women, 70, 89–90, 95, 116
Great commission, the, 11, 20, 23, 43–46, 78, 101, 119